This book may be kept
...AVS

W9-AQT-220

CONTINENTAL STAGECRAFT

The Redoutensaal, a great and splendid eighteenth-century ballroom in the Hofburg in Vienna, with an arrangement of curved walls, staircases and platforms newly built into one end. Here, under the light of crystal chandeliers, surrounded by the baroque beauty of Maria Theresa's palace, audience and players unite in a relationship freed from all the associations of modern stage-setting, a relationship essentially theatrical in the newest and the oldest sense of the word. The stage is here shown cleared of all but a few chairs for the wedding scene in Mozart's *The Marriage of Figaro.*

CONTINENTAL STAGECRAFT

KENNETH MACGOWAN
ROBERT EDMOND JONES

PN 2570
M 14 c

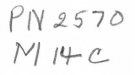

ST. JOSEPH'S UNIVERSITY STX
PN2570.M14c
Continental stagecraft

3 9353 00093 7324

61383

BENJAMIN BLOM, INC.

New York

First published N. Y., 1922
Reissued by arrangement with Mrs. Macgowan
by Benjamin Blom, Inc., 1964
L. C. Catalog Card No.: 64-14711

Printed in U.S.A. by
NOBLE OFFSET PRINTERS, INC.
NEW YORK 3, N. Y.

TO THE
PLAYWRIGHTS
OF AMERICA

Certain of the chapters and illustrations of *Continental Stagecraft* have appeared in *Vanity Fair, The Century Magazine, Arts and Decoration, T h e Bookman, The Theatre Magazine, Harper's Bazar, The Theatre Arts Magazine, The Freeman,* and *Shadowland.*

PREFATORY NOTE

THIS book is a record of impressions gained from ten weeks of travel through the theaters of France, Sweden, Germany, Czecho-Slovakia, and Austria during April, May, and June, 1922. These impressions are partly reinforced, partly orientated, through previous visits to Paris and London, and through a long sojourn of Mr. Jones in Germany just before the war.

For the purposes of this book, the journey excluded England, because observation and reliable report showed little there that was not a faint echo of what was to be found on the Continent. Russia was regretfully excluded for reasons of time and the difficulties of travel; but fortunately we were able to see in Stockholm a performance by the touring company of the Moscow Art Theater. Though the most interesting evenings of our trip were spent in the Redoutensaal in Vienna, and in the Vieux-Colombier and the Cirque Medrano in Paris, the larger part of our time was passed in Germany, and the greater number of illustrations come from productions seen there. In Berlin, in particular, there were things to be seen which had been much discussed by American visitors—*Masse-Mensch*, the Grosses Schauspielhaus, and the work of Leopold Jessner,—

and these, we felt, demanded lengthy study and analysis.

In our ten weeks Mr. Jones and I saw close to sixty performances. We had expected to find it difficult, if not impossible,
to see in this time as much as we should have liked of the really
significant new work of the Continental theater. But, as it
happened, good fortune and the great courtesy shown us everywhere enabled us to see almost everything that we wished.
Through special performances arranged by the managements
of the Royal Swedish Opera and the Berlin Volksbühne, and
by Jacques Copeau, director of the Vieux-Colombier, we saw
half a dozen most important productions which we might otherwise have missed. Luck and the repertory system found us at
various German theaters in time to witness the most characteristic and significant work of the past few years. Finally, we
were fortunate enough to come upon two theaters—one accomplished, the other potential—of extraordinary interest
and importance, which had not as yet been seen or discussed
by American visitors, the Redoutensaal in Vienna and the
Cirque Medrano in Paris. *Continental Stagecraft* cannot
pretend to be so exhaustive a study as a year's visit would have
made possible, but, in view of the exceptional circumstances, I
think that it is more than proportionately representative.

With the exception of one sketch of a supposititious production in the Cirque Medrano, the illustrations show exactly what
we saw and nothing else. Mr. Jones's drawings are in them-

selves a kind of criticism which the modern theater stands much in need of. They give the actual visual quality of the best productions on the Continental stage far better than could photographs of settings and actors, which are usually flashlights innocent of the atmosphere produced by the stage lighting, or the designs of the scenic artists, which are sometimes imperfectly realized and sometimes bettered in actual production. Mr. Jones made his drawings as soon as might be after the performance, working from many rough notes made during the progress of the play. They are, I believe, uncommonly true to the impression gained by the audience. My only reservation would be that they catch the scene and the lighting always at the best moment, and, through the quality of the drawing, they sometimes add a beauty that is perhaps a little flattering to the original.

The text is a collaboration in ideas, though not, with the exception of the captions under the pictures, in writing. It is a compilation of our impressions, reactions, and conclusions. Because the words are my own, I have taken the liberty of the personal pronoun "I" when "we" would be editorially pompous or inexact.

The book began as an attempt to supplement the International Theater Exhibition held in Amsterdam and London during the first half of 1922. This large, varied, and arresting collection of sketches and models showed the art of the theater largely as it existed in the imaginations of the stage designers. Many of these sketches were for productions never made, some had been greatly altered for better or for worse in the course of production. It was our feeling that we might be able to add something to the knowledge which this important exhibition was spreading abroad if we could make some record, however incomplete, of the actual accomplishment of the artists upon the stage, and particularly of the directors and actors, who, after all, have the major share in the art of the theater.

We have seen so much that is interesting, so much that is significant, and a few things so stimulating and inspiriting, that we have been tempted often to push our report of impressions into an anticipation of future progress. We have, I fear, substituted our own imaginations in many places for those of the artists of the International Exhibition.

KENNETH MACGOWAN.

Pelham Manor, N. Y.,
   1 August, 1922.

TABLE OF CONTENTS

TABLE OF CONTENTS

LIST OF ILLUSTRATIONS

xv

LIST OF ILLUSTRATIONS

CONTINENTAL STAGECRAFT

CONTINENTAL STAGECRAFT

CHAPTER I

BEYOND REALISM

IT is a pity to begin a book by being dull. But a time of change is upon us in the theater, and a time of change is a time for definitions.

We have passed through such times before, and we have come out after some years—a century or so—with categories neatly fixed. We can look back along the history of English literature and place a judicial finger there and there and there and say Middle English, Classicism, Romanticism. All this is pretty well set. Then we come to Realism and its quagmires —quagmires of balked creation and quagmires of discussion —and we wallow about gesticulating and shouting and splashing the mud into our immortal eyes. What is this bog we have been so busy in? And what is the fitful and rather blinding storm of illumination which plays about the horizon and calls itself Expressionism?

Of course these things are just what we care to make them. Various parties to the argument choose various definitions—

3

the kinds that suit their themes. I claim no more for mine than that they will make clear what I am talking about, and save a certain amount of futile dispute.

There are plenty of sources of confusion in discussions about art. To begin with, it is not an easy thing to limit a dynamic organism by definition. Creative efforts in drama, fiction or painting run out of one category and into another with distressing ease. More than that, there are apt to be many parts to a whole, many divisions to a category; and the parts or the divisions can be extraordinarily different. Finally, fanatics and tea-table gossips are equally unscrupulous when it comes to "proving" a point. They make the definitions of friends and foes mean what they like. They take the part for the whole, the division for the category. They pin down a lively and meandering work of art at just the place where they want it. Two disputants, bent on exhibiting the more indecent side of human intelligence, can make the twilight of discussion into a pit of black confusion.

Let us bring the thing down to the present quarrel in the theater: the quarrel with Realism, which has moments of clarity; the quarrel with Expressionism, which is murky as hell.

What are we going to mean when we talk about Realism? So far as this book goes, the word Realism means a way of looking at life which came into vogue about fifty years ago.

It sees truth as representation. It demands a more or less literal picture of people and happenings. It insists that human beings upon the stage shall say or do only those things that are reasonably plausible in life. Resemblance is not always its end, but resemblance is a test that must be satisfied before any other quality may be admitted. Realism is not, of course, a matter of trousers, silk hats, and machinery. The realistic attitude can invade the sixteenth century, as it does in Hauptmann's *Florian Geyer*. Trousers, silk hats, and machinery can be the properties of a non-realistic play like O'Neill's *The Hairy Ape*. The test of Realism, as the term is here employed, is the test of plausibility: Would men and women talk in this fashion in real life under the conditions of time, place, and action supplied by the playwright? It is the business of the realistic playwright to draw as much as possible of inner truth to the surface without distorting the resemblance to actuality.

There should not be a great deal to quarrel about in such a definition of Realism, though its adherents may deny hotly the natural assertion that the method of Realism is barren either in whole or in part. At any rate, people generally understand what the row is about, and the disputants can kick up only about so much dust on this battle-field. Non-realism is another matter.

That the thing is the opposite of Realism is obvious in just one respect: It does not admit the test of resemblance. It denies in the theater, as furiously as do the works of Cézanne or Picasso in the picture gallery, the validity of representation. But what will it substitute for the technique of Realism and what will it call the substitute? It will go back to romantic periods for a free technique, but it will look forward for its materials along paths which psychological research has lately opened to men and women outside the ranks of true poetic genius. By this it may arrive at the inner truth of Shelley and Goethe, Shakespeare and Æschylus, while it sacrifices the outer truth of Ibsen and Bataille, Pinero and Galsworthy. The question is both of technique and of materials, for an inner truth is to be found in a study of the unconscious mind which will not brook the obstructions of actuality and resemblance. Inner truth is so much more important than actuality that the new type of drama will not bother itself to achieve both, and if one must infringe on the other—which must happen in almost every case—then it chooses quickly and fearlessly the inner truth.

To give this anti-Realism a name involves confusions dear to the heart of the controversialist. To give it the name Expressionism multiplies these confusions. Yet it is hard to see any alternative at the moment. We must embrace the name—and the confusions.

The chief confusion is due to the fact that there are two kinds of Expressionism, as there are doubtless two kinds of Realism. There is the larger and there is the smaller. Realism can be a mere technique—resemblance; and it can also be a resemblance through which you catch a vision of the soul. Expressionism can be seen by the friends of Realism only as the narrow, neurotic, violent, and formless art which displays itself in the dramas of the new German writers like Georg Kaiser. I should be prepared to defend this sort of Expressionism against the Realism of Augustus Thomas or even of John Galsworthy; but I should not admit that it was the end of the reaction against resemblance. Expressionism may be applied—and for the purposes of this book it shall be applied —to the whole tendency against Realism, just as Romanticism is applied to the whole tendency against Classicism. Many who dislike Realism and neurotic German Expressionism equally, prefer to give the form they seek some such well-worn and inoffensive label as Poetry. This finickiness doesn't matter—except as it admits new confusions and dodges the issue. This issue is plain and should be kept plain. Realism, in any but a very extraordinary sense, is a cramp upon art. Instinctively artists of the theater are beginning to recognize this and to seek some way out. This involves new qualities in the play. For practical purposes let us call the way of escape Expressionism. Some other term may establish itself in the course of years, but for the moment this is all we have.

It is fairly easy to apply these terms and definitions to the current theater—if you are not too doctrinaire or too partizan.

Realism yawningly enfolds ninety-nine out of a hundred playwrights. Maeterlinck and D'Annunzio require a little special attention and Shaw and Barrie raise nice points. But, in general, the distinction holds; resemblance shepherds the realistic plays, emanations of the unconscious guide us to the expressionistic. Even the purely representational performances which most of our actors and directors give do not always succeed in hiding the cleavage.

The most startling and disturbing experience that any friend of Expressionism can have is to sit through a performance of Tchehoff's *The Cherry Orchard* by the Moscow Art Theater —even by that portion of Stanislavsky's celebrated company which was cut off by Wrangel's army while playing in Southern Russia and compelled to tour Europe for two years before repatriation was possible. Here is a play of a generation ago written by the man whose dramas were the cornerstone of success for the world's greatest realistic theater. It is a *genre* study almost without plot: decayed aristocrats, old servants, newly-rich peasants and the incident of the sale for debt of an ancestral property. There is no more violence in it than the violence of life which rots an oak. There is no more distortion than is to be expected in light reflected from the troubled surface of life. And it is played with an almost utter perfection of realistic detail, complete impersonation, and rounded ensemble.

8

Yet if this is Realism we have never known Realism in our theater. It carries us through life and out on the other side. It drenches us with a mystic sense of existence. And when we read the text of the play and separate it from the extraordinary emotional actuality of the performance, we discover again and again and again speech that drives straight at free expression instead of resemblance, and action and character permeated with an almost religious symbolism. All this fused by playwright and players into what seems a work of the most perfect resemblance, but what is actually only the appearance of appearance.

The surface of the play is the surface of life. Mme. Ranevsky has returned to her estates after a turmoil of years in France. There are the usual appendages: a daughter, an adopted daughter, a governess, a housemaid, a major-domo, and a man-servant who have grown into the life of the house, a brother, an old, impoverished friend, a village clerk with his eye on the maid-servant, an up-and-coming merchant whose grandfather was a serf on the estate. These people talk a great deal, and in talking they make certain matters plain. One of these is that no one can save the estate, the beautiful cherry orchard, from the consequences of the family temperament. Madame and her brother have always spent their money as becomes gentlefolk, and some one has forgotten the secret of how the cherries used to be dried and sent to the markets of the far cities every year. They flounder about in self-deception, always hoping for succor, never willing to accept the scheme of the friendly merchant for cutting the estate up into villa lots, and never able to do anything themselves to save it from the auctioneer. Ultimately the merchant buys it in, and in blissful callousness puts the ax to the trees as the family leave the old house. Out of these people and their dilemma rises the most curious and moving symbolism. A suggestion of symbols, rather; for there is nothing bald about it. Truths of Russian temperament, even Russian politics, are figured with the hidden yet revealing quality that so often rises out of life like an odor from old fields, freighted with memories and anticipations. Perhaps the simplest and most moving example of this comes at the very end of the play. Through it all has moved a mumbling, bent old man who has been the loving guardian of the household for two generations, one of those rare and ancient servants who, by sheer servility, have lifted themselves out of servantage and into a share in the family life. In the end, the house is sold, the furniture removed, the shutters closed. The family depart. Then into the dim room comes the old man, forgotten. He totters across to the derelict sofa that has been left behind. He curls up on it like some old leaf. There in the darkness he dies. The soul of old Russia.

As the old man dies something occurs that gives us all the license we need in order to see in other portions of the play

Realistic production at its best. The final moment
of Tchehoff's *The Cherry Orchard* as produced
by the touring company of the Moscow Art
Theatre. The ancestral house has been sold, curtains and pictures have been taken down, the furniture is shrouded. The shutters are closed. The lights
are so dim that the room is no longer a room but
a vague, brooding presence. The old servant
gropes his way through the darkness, crawls upon
the couch and dies.

methods and attitudes far indeed from Realism. The stage directions read: "A distant sound is heard, as if from the sky, and the sound of a string breaking, dying away, melancholy." It is a sound that occurs also in the second act, unexplained, ominous. Symbolism. Arbitrary and very expressive sounds from heaven. Is it at all surprising to find the characters of this play indulging in lengthy accounts of their lives without taking the least trouble to find some stranger who might plausibly be ignorant of it all?

Perhaps this is Realism, perhaps not. Certainly it is both sharp with actuality and mystic with life's intensity as these Russian players act it. The company did not contain the greatest of the group which Stanislavsky has gathered about him since he opened his theater in 1897. The director himself was not there to play the maundering brother. On this night Kachaloff was out of the cast. But Mme. Knipper, the widow of Tchehoff, played Mme. Ranevsky, and P. A. Pavloff played the old servant. How many of the other players acted parts long familiar to them I cannot say; but their work gave the impression not only of exceptionally fine individual performances but of an ensemble long and lovingly built up into perfection. It is an old *cliché* as well as a sad comment on acting as an art to say that a player does not *play* a character but literally *is* the character. In the case of this company from the Moscow Art Theater, there is a deep intensity in the perform-

11

ance and a frank desire for absolute impersonation which make such a comment on their playing of *The Cherry Orchard* the obvious and revealing truth. It is a comment that applies to the ensemble as much as to the individual acting.

The wedding of an utterly realistic performance with a play of mystic overtones is justified by the sense of an old and complete life which both possess. The intimacy of the actors with one another is as evident as the intimacy of the characters they play, and the intimacy of masters and servants in this Russian family. The welcome of the mistress on her return may be a matter of the clever rehearsal of off-stage noise—amazingly clever, you can believe; but when this adoration comes out of the wings and walks upon the stage, it is seen as the perfection of emotion and impersonation. A performance in so foreign a tongue as Russian gains because our eager imagination is at work to interpret in the acting the gaps left by the lack of words. It also loses, because the meaning of the play is not always there to show the linking of character and character, and of incident and incident; great spaces of action are blank and without emotion; we carry away fewer and shorter memories. How many and how continuous, however, are the memories of this performance, and how piercingly keen are the sharpest of them! Mme Knipper: a welling flood of emotion at the old nursery of her childhood; blind affection for the lovely, ancient orchard; childlike prodigality in her gesture as she scatters money that might once have saved the estate, followed by child-like penitence; and then the moment when she hears at last that the orchard is sold, when her ability to ignore and forget slips from her and she turns old before our eyes. Pavloff, prince of impersonators of old men, hobbling about the room; a bent and shuffling figure eternally mumbling, eternally nursing; a watery-eyed kiss for madame's hand, a pat for the twisted collar of the brother, a touch to the turn of a curtain; an old, old, devoted shape speaking its fullness of character in every movement. Other figures almost as fully felt and seen. Each one doing the least little thing with an arresting significance. Here for once are actors who realize the importance of crossing a stage, as a display not of themselves but of their characters. Here, equally, are actors who have got by all the small egoisms of their kind. It is said that Stanislavsky found his players among artists, writers, students, shopkeepers, anywhere but in "the profession." At any rate in twenty years he has made them into selfless but distinguished parts of a new organism. Their intimacy as people must be as great as the intimacy which they give their characters on the stage. They are an orchestra; their playing is a music, a harmony. They seem to have lived into this play in the eighteen years that they have given it until now they are part one of another. It does not matter that some may have had their rôles only five years, perhaps only five months. They are enveloped in the mother-

13

liquor of this mature, well-aged performance. You recall the stew that Anatole France described: "To be good it must have been cooking lengthily upon a gentle fire. Clemence's stew has been cooking for twenty years. She puts into the pot sometimes goose or bacon, sometimes sausage or beans, but it is always the same stew. The foundation endures; this ancient and precious foundation gives the stew the quality that in the pictures of old Venetian masters you find in the women's flesh."

Such Realism as this of the Moscow Art Theater compares most curiously with the best we know of realistic acting in the productions of David Belasco and Arthur Hopkins. It has the care and minutiæ of Belasco sharpened by far greater ability on the part of players and director, and mellowed by time. It has the naturalness of Hopkins; but, because it is secured by deliberate direction and not by the indirection of the American's method, the naturalness fits into a general design and is never slipshod. (So far Stanislavsky denies life and its accidents!) It is, of course, worse than futile to compare such acting with our own for any purpose but understanding. We cannot achieve a performance of this kind so long as we have no permanent companies, no repertory system. It is not alone a matter of the leisurely method of production which Stanislavsky can employ,—months spent in study of the script, long readings and discussions over every character. Repertory keeps the actors playing a piece for years. They are not re-peating themselves evening after evening with mechanical de-votion. They come back to the play from other parts. They see it anew. If it is such a piece as *The Cherry Orchard*, they plunge into its depths with a sense of refreshment. They are the parts of a whole which they can never greatly alter, but which they can enrich by new contributions.

We have, then, in this performance an almost perfect exam-ple of minute and thorough Realism, fused into something beyond Realism through its union with a play distinctly ex-pressionistic in certain qualities. It would be easy to see how frank, non-realistic acting could be applied to *The Cherry Orchard*. It is, in fact, very hard to see how the players can act some of the speeches as they do, notably the descriptions of themselves and their lives which the governess and Madame Ranevsky furnish to fellow-characters fully acquainted with all they say, characters who very rightly pay not the slightest heed. If ever a player had an opportunity to bridge directly the gap which has existed between stage and audience for the past fifty years, and to present emotion as simply and honestly and theatrically as do the gravestones in Spoon River, it is the actress who plays the governess. She begins the second act with the following speech, virtually a soliloquy, to which none of the others on the stage pay the least attention, even the atten-tion of boredom:

15

I have no proper passport. I don't know how old I am; I always feel I am still young. When I was a little girl my father and mother used to go about from one country fair to another, giving performances, and very good ones, too. I used to do the *salto mortale* and all sorts of tricks. When papa and mamma died, an old German lady adopted me and educated me. Good! When I grew up I became a governess. But where I come from and who I am I haven't a notion. Who my parents were—very likely they weren't married—I don't know. I don't know anything about it. I long to talk so, and I have no one to talk to, I have no friends or relations.

Is this Realism? Is it Expressionism? Is it something between, some Realism of the Spirit opposed to the Realism of Flesh which we know? Can we say that we know true Realism of the Flesh as yet? Even if we do know it in a few fugitive productions, are we ready to give up not only such Realism but also the possibility of deeply moving performances like this of *The Cherry Orchard*, and to go seeking a fresh and debatable thing far on the other side of experience? If we are, it is because we see that such perfection as this of *The Cherry Orchard* is a very rare thing for which we pay with hours of the commonplace, and because we recognize that when a play reaches such spiritual quality it has traveled so far from Realism that the journey is almost over.

CHAPTER II

THE LIVING STAGE

THERE is something in the nature of the theater that makes Realism a natural and a thoroughly unsatisfactory method of expression. Its principal material, the actor, is too near actuality. It is no triumph of art to make a flesh-and-blood man named Grant Mitchell into a flesh-and-blood man named Andrew Lane. Especially when the heart of the whole business is an elaborate pretense that there really isn't any actor, and there really isn't any theater, and we are really looking through the fourth wall of a room in the next village.

Obviously no other art is so close to life or so quick with life's vitality. Literature uses printed signs of a very arbitrary and formal nature, which we translate into words forming ideas and mental pictures, which, in turn, may suggest human beings and their emotions. Music employs sounds some of which faintly suggest bird-notes or the rumble of the heavens, but none of which comes within shouting distance of the human voice. Painting has pieces of canvas and lumps of colored clays, and these it arranges in patterns, through which, by

17

custom and habit, we are able to gain an impression of a curiously flattened life. Even sculpture, literal as its rounded, three-dimensional shapes ordinarily are, must use the intermediary of clay or rock. The theater is the one art that works in the materials of life itself. It employs life to render life. Painting, architecture, and sculpture may supply a background to the actor, but the actor is the center of the play, and when he speaks the words of literature he speaks them as the actual human being from whom they are supposed to come.

The actor brings the theater far too close to life to please some of its great lovers. The actuality of the actor affrights them. Gordon Craig, once an actor and always a true partizan of the theater, has felt this. He has found the actor too much a piece of life, too much a creature of the emotions of existence, and too little an impersonal and dependable tool of the artist. "The actions of the actor's body, the expression of his face, the sounds of his voice, all are at the mercy of the winds of his emotions." He is not clay, he is not stone, he is not curves of ink, he is not arbitrary sounds produced from wood or brass. He is life itself, and a very irregular and undependable part of life. Therefore, says Craig, the thing that the actor gives us is not a work of art; "it is a series of accidental confessions."

Now the contrast between the pliant and well-behaved

clay and the intractable actor is interesting. And there is a certain significance in the fact that when Craig describes the work of the actor as a series of "accidental confessions," he uses a phrase which would delight the harshest of the realists—the writers who practised Naturalism, the literal transcription of the irregularities of life. But the issue goes deeper. The actor is essential to the theater. He cannot be turned out for a glorified puppet, an *Ubermarionette*. But perhaps he can be told that he is far too near life and its accidents to spend his time imitating them. To give us life and its significance the dramatist, like workers in the other arts, needs an intermediary. If the actor is not a true intermediary, because he is a part of life, the dramatist has only to see that he can go beyond the actuality of the physical actor to Form. With the creative vitality of the living actor to awaken us and make us sensitive and responsive, the dramatist may strive to reach beyond outward truth to that inner truth which presents itself to us in deliberate and natural arrangements of life.

It is no easy thing to tell what is meant by the word Form when we take it past the idea of the design of things in a literal sense, and apply it to significance in the design of life. But it is easy to say that Form has nothing whatever to do with representation or illusion. As Clive Bell points out in his book *Art*, in which he makes a brilliant plea for

19

what he calls "significant form" as the test of visual art, the fact that a thing is representative, does not at all suggest either the presence or the absence of Form. It does not preclude its having Form just as it does not in the least assure it. The theater will always have the physical body of the actor, and to that extent it will always be representational. But that is certainly all it need have of illusion. What the actor says and the atmosphere in which he appears may be absolutely non-representational. Even his physical body, as he uses it, may take on qualities outside and beyond illusion.

It remains the dramatist's special business to master the extremely difficult task of fighting through to Form while retaining the realistic technique, or else—which seems far better—frankly to desert Realism, representation, illusion, and write directly in significant terms, no matter how unplausible they may be. After all, common sense sees that it is better to concentrate all of an artist's technical energies on the major thing he wishes to accomplish. Bell says of the men and women of the future: "When they think of the early twentieth-century painters they will think only of the artists who tried to create Form—the artisans who tried to create illusions will be forgotten." It is equally true that the artist who tries to create illusion is more than likely to forget to create Form.

Now creating Form does not mean hiding the actuality of the actor under strange robes. There seems to be a curious notion abroad that the alternative to Realism is Romance. It is true that in trying to escape out of Realism a number of playwrights have avoided reality and wandered into the never-never-land of Thalanna and Kongros. It is also true that modern sciences, history, archeology, and psychology, have made the past new and real and alive again, and that certain playwrights have seen in the rejuvenated ages a chance to escape the realistic and to attain more permanent values. But it is not true that the present offers smaller opportunities. Expressionist playwrights have already shown this conclusively enough; witness Eugene O'Neill's *The Hairy Ape*.

Theatrical history has never been as popular with theatrical reformers as it should be. It shows not only that the realistic technique is a matter of the last half century, and that the greatest periods of the theater's history were non-realistic. But it shows also that even when Realism was an impossible idea, and when expressive, significant Form was the only thing at which the playwright aimed, the theater and its audiences usually lived frankly and healthfully in the present.

Greek tragedy, to be sure, was not a thing of the present —except in the reality of its religious emotion. Its heroes came out of the past. They did not talk or act like the Athenians that watched them. They even dressed according

21

to a set convention of their own. In every way the Greek tragic theater embraced Form, directly and naturally. It was in the temperament of the Greeks. Their sculpture was realistic to a degree never before reached and not surpassed in physical truth to-day; yet from these statues we gain a sense of Form far more significant than the sense of life which they give us. Representation was not an end to the Greek artist. The dramatist of Athens felt no desire to "humanize" his heroes or to make them like the people about him in any particular. The drama was religious in origin and had not yet grown temporal. So long as the Greek mind had its fondness for Form, there could be no demand for the smallest actuality.

But man's natural fondness for "humanness" and "recognition" found plenty of opportunity for expression after the passing of the great Greeks. And it was satisfied in almost every case without breaking in too sharply on the heart of the drama, expression of Form. The medieval religious drama was both religious and temporal. The saints were very much of the times in clothes and in habits. The Bible characters lived the lives and wore the garments and exercised the minds of people of the Middle Ages. Shakespeare dipped back into history and into romance, too, but his Italian nobles dressed like Londoners, his Roman "mechanicals" were British workmen, and his Athenian yokels came out of

22

the English countryside. Molière "modernized" the Roman rascal Phormio into the Neapolitan rascal Scapin, and the ordinary Parisian gentleman served him for Alceste. Phèdre and Iphigénie were not so very Greek. In England trage-dians played Shakespeare in the costumes of their own day down through Garrick, Siddons, and Kemble. And do you imagine that all this had the slightest effect on the plays, any bearing on their expression of the inner Form rather than the outward shape of life? In spite of the flesh-and-blood actor, clothed in the costumes of the time, the playwright was saved from mere representation, from all this peep-hole business of Realism. Doubtless he was saved because the temper of his time was not corrupted and twisted and tortured by the unholy union of science and capitalism. But it is rather interesting to remember that the actors appeared in theaters so utterly unreal, so essentially theatrical, that nobody could imagine for a moment that he was standing with his eye glued to a chink in the fourth wall.

The theaters of the past united the temporal and the eter-nal, the passing moment and the permanent Form partly in innocence, and partly from a natural ability to understand things better in their own terms. We, too, can grasp more of the Form of life if we see it derived from the life we know. But this does not mean that the Elizabethans had the slightest interest in the thing that has absorbed our stage—

plausibility, representation, resemblance. To-day we are beginning again to desire reality of soul instead of mere reality of body. We want to know about our own time and our own people, but we don't give a hang to learn how imperfectly, how haltingly, a modern, realistic Hamlet would express his thoughts on suicide.

It is easy enough to see how much Shakespeare's greatest tragedy would have lost if he had written like a Galsworthy. Poetry of word is not the only thing that would have gone by the board. Poetry of idea would have disappeared, too. More than that, the ability of a character to express himself would have been hideously confined within the formula of plausibility. Perhaps so great an artist could have written his tragedy without permitting a single person to speak an inner thought that time and circumstance could not bring out, but I am a little inclined to doubt it. And I am very much inclined to assert that the vitality and the effectiveness of such a work of unnatural and straining effort would have been nothing beside the vitality and effectiveness of the *Hamlet* we know.

For twenty years the European stage has struggled over the problem of plausibility and resemblance in setting. The thing called the new movement in the theater has spent half the time devising mechanisms and technique for achieving genuine representation instead of the bastard thing that tried

24

George Pitoëff's arrangement of *He Who Gets
Slapped* in Paris. The stage is draped in black
curtains. Narrow scarlet ribbons looped from the
proscenium arch indicate a circus tent. The actors
make their entrances and exists from behind a
huge circus poster, which is changed from act to
act.

to make a dining room out of badly painted and flimsy canvas. And it has spent about half the time trying to get rid of this machinery and this technique in order to escape the Realism which demanded such things. In Stockholm you see the touring company of the Moscow Art Theater playing realistic plays in just the sort of ugly, cheap, old setting that Craig, Reinhardt and Belasco equally set their faces against. In Dresden you see Shaw's *Pygmalion* played at the State Schauspielhaus in settings as solid and illusive as stone and wood. In Paris you see the Russian Georges Pitoëff giving Andreyeff's *He Who Gets Slapped* in black curtains with four ribbons looped up to indicate the form of a circus tent, and Tchehoff's *The Seagull* in settings which go back to the old flapping canvas flats again, admitting that the theater is a place of pretense, and which then attempt—not very successfully—to give these flats, in color and outline, the Form of the play.

Still further along the way from Realism to an expressionist stage, you find Copeau's naked stage in Paris that unites frankly with the auditorium, and changes very little from *The S. S. Tenacity* to *Les Frères Karamazov*. Finally in Vienna, you find, in the Redoutensaal made from the ballroom of Maria Theresa's palace, a theater without proscenium, machinery or scenery, a theater where the actor is frankly the actor. Here you have the culminating expression of the growing sense

25

in Europe that, because the stage is so close to life in the presence of the living actor, it need not and it must not attempt to create the illusion of reality. Through such a conception the theater is freed once more to seek the Form of life.

CHAPTER III

THE PATH OF THE PLAY

THE story of the attempt of the theater to escape from Realism is a curious story. As a deliberate effort of the playwrights to see life in the terms of Form instead of accidental actuality it goes back only half a dozen years through the dramas of the Germans who adopted the word Expressionism to describe their aim and technique. It has hung potential for ten or fifteen years in the work of the more advanced and philosophic designers and directors of the new stagecraft, a waiting stimulus to the playwrights. As an unconscious impulse to reach beyond the limits of Realism its beginnings are to be traced back twenty, thirty, almost forty years in the work of some of Europe's ablest realists.

The two greatest figures in the modern theater—which is the realistic theater—give the same demonstration of the limitations of Realism, and turn in the same fashion away from actuality and towards an intense spiritual vitality. Both Ibsen and Strindberg come out of Romanticism into Realism, and pass on into a Symbolism that is far on the way towards Expressionism. In Ibsen the new tendency is clearly marked in

27

The Wild Duck (1884) and develops gradually through *The Master Builder* (1892) to completion in *When We Dead Awaken* (1899). Strindberg's *Towards Damascus* (1898) carries strong hints of the spiritual intensity which threatened the outer reality of so many of Strindberg's earlier plays; and by 1902, in *Swanwhite* and *The Dream Play*, he is well embarked on a type of non-realistic drama which finds a bizarre culmination in *The Spook Sonata* in 1907.

Two other European playwrights of distinction—Tchehoff and Wedekind—show a similar dissatisfaction with pure Realism, though neither passes through the three stages of development to be traced in Ibsen and Strindberg. The work of Tchehoff and the work of Wedekind is all pretty much of a piece. It is never wholly realistic in the narrowest sense. Each has a peculiar quality and method throughout. Tchehoff, beginning in 1896 with *The Seagull*, keeps to a Realism of such intense spiritual truth that, in a performance of his *The Cherry Orchard* by the Moscow Art Theater such as I have described, its extraordinary virtues are the virtues of Expressionism. Wedekind's first play, the thesis-drama *The Awakening of Spring*, written in 1891, is stamped with his curious and violent intensity, and his sense of the spiritual overtones of life. In 1895 and 1903 he produced in the two parts of *Lulu*—*Erdgeist* and *Pandora's Box*—dramas horrifically actual in their pictures of sexual aberration and at the same time

28

so intense psychologically and so sharply defined and apt in action that their Realism treads close on the boundaries which Expressionism has over-passed.

There is a curious distinction in end and means between such plays as these of Ibsen, Strindberg, Tchehoff, and Wedekind, and the newer expressionist dramas of Germany and America. The earlier plays indulge in symbolic, fantastic, deeply spiritual ideas, but their language is almost always highly realistic. They are still bound to the past of their authors and to the present of their theater. The newer expressionist dramas, on the other hand, are as free in speech as they are in idea. It is a freedom that often makes a harmonious wedding of end and means. Sometimes, as in plays of *Der Sturm* group, the language is so completely free from the bonds of actuality that it approaches the onomatopoetic verse of Mallarmé depending on sound for its sense. In Eugene O'Neill's distinguished piece of Expressionism, *The Hairy Ape*, the playwright strikes a happy medium with speech which is realistic and characteristic in idiom but which is developed in idea, intensity and length of utterance clean past the possibilities of the people of the play. Occasionally you find a pseudo-expressionist piece like *Vatermord*, by Arnold Bronnen, whose action is naturalistic—grossly naturalistic—but whose language is often far from natural. This piece was first produced in Berlin in the summer of 1922 when the mind of the German capital could safely be described as neurotic. Its subject matter—the incest and patricide of the Œdipus complex, with a little adventitious homosexuality, all circling about a boy in his 'teens —produced a stormy session between adherents and opponents, a session finally ended by the *Schutzpolizei* with rifles and the command: "Sei ruhig, meine Herrschaften!" The run which followed at one of the theaters formerly directed by Max Reinhardt may be explained by the notorious subject matter, but there were critics to assert that Bronnen had a style of considerable power as well as novelty. The boy's final speech, as he staggers onto the stage from an inner room, where he has killed his father, and rebuffs the passionate entreaties of his mother, is translated from the printed version, retaining the one form of punctuation used, the slanting dash to indicate the end of a line, though not necessarily of a sentence:

I'm through with you / I'm through with everything / Go bury your husband you are old / I am young / I don't know you / I am free /
Nobody in front of me nobody next to me nobody over me father's dead / Heaven I spring up to you. I fly / It pounds shakes groans complains must rise swells wells up springs up flies must rise must rise

I

I bloom

Before such an arrangement of words *The Spook Sonata* seems almost mid-Victorian. The Student speaks to the ghostly

30

Milkmaid in the most matter of fact fashion. Even the old Mummy, the mad woman who always sits in a closet, talks like a most realistic parrot when she is not talking like a most realistic woman. Here it is the ideas that stagger and affright you, the molding minds, the walking Dead, the cook who draws all the nourishment out of the food before she serves it, the terrible relations of young and old; all of them are things having faint patterns in actuality and raised by Strindberg to a horrible clarity.

To follow the banner of Expressionism in playwriting—I say nothing of stage setting, for that is, happily, another matter—requires all three Graces and a strong stomach. The bizarre morbidity, the nauseating sexuality, the lack of any trace of joy or beauty, which characterize the work of most of those who labeled themselves expressionists in Germany during the past few years, match Strindberg at his unhappiest, while the vigor with which they drive their ideas forth in speech far outdoes him. Expressionism, in the narrow sense in which such plays define it, is a violent storm of emotion beating up from the unconscious mind. It is no more than the waves which shatter themselves on the shore of our conscious existence, only a distorted hint of the deep and mysterious sea of the unconscious. Expressionism, as we have so far known it, is a meeting of the fringes of the conscious and the unconscious, and the meeting is startling indeed.

31

Germany's reception of the expressionist plays was open-minded, as is Germany's reception of almost all new effort. The dramas of the best of the expressionists—Georg Kaiser and Walter Hasenclever—were produced in leading theaters, on the official stages of Dresden and of Frankfort, and in Reinhardt's playhouses, for example. But by the summer of 1922 they had disappeared from the very catholic and long-suffering repertories of these houses, and while Wedekind and Strindberg were produced from Stockholm to Vienna, the simon-pure expressionists, the playwrights of what I think it is fair to call the lesser Expressionism, were hardly to be seen. Only the one-act opera, *Mörder, Hoffnung der Frauen*, a composition by Paul Hindemith on a playlet by the artist-author, Oskar Kokoschka, was being played.

This piece, produced at the City Opera House in Frankfort, points an interesting union and parallel between at least one sort of Expressionism and music. The action, passing in some indefinite olden time, is symbolically very difficult—quite as difficult as its title, *Murderer, Hope of Women*. The emotion of the scenes, on the other hand, is clear enough, and it receives from the music a background of color, a tonal reinforcement, that is most welcome; at the same time the composer finds in the vigorous and intense, if somewhat arbitrary, feeling of the playwright a provocative challenge.

Kokoschka himself designed a setting for *Mörder, Hoff-*

A setting by Ludwig Sievert for *Mörder, Hoff-nung der Frauen*, an expressionistic opera by Kokoschka. Ramps lead from the center of the stage to raised platforms right and left. Dark walls rise at the back, broken by triangular entrances at either side and by a grilled doorway in the center, flanked by tall triangular pylons of red-orange.

nung der Frauen when it was first produced at the Albert Theater in Dresden as a play. A photograph of the production betrays an uneasy setting, hardly stage-worthy in arrangement and composition, and rather badly executed. The pages of *Die Neue Schaubühne* have shown several other expressionist stage designs as unsatisfactory, but in the more widely known productions these pieces have been lucky enough to fall into the hands of first-rate men like Adolf Linnebach of Dresden and Ludwig Sievert of Frankfort. Sketches made from Linnebach's production of Hasenclever's *Jenseits* in Dresden show a simple and effective use of light and shadow and of little else, with certain necessary elements of design projected by a sort of magic-lantern technique upon the background of dome or curtain. In actual performance Sievert's setting for the Kokoschka opera is strong and arresting with dark surfaces massed in triangles symbolic of the feminine element dominant in the piece, and with a successful, if not very subtle, use of red and red-orange on the pylon surfaces guarding the prison door. The direction of the singers and chorus, under the hand of Dr. Ernst Lert, is a thoroughly expressive part of music and setting.

Though the most celebrated plays of the expressionist pioneers have failed to make a place for themselves in the German repertory, they have had their effect. Playwrights who might have written in the conventional mode have been

33

turned towards a freer technique, and they have succeeded in accomplishing interesting and promising things. The most notable of the plays thus produced, *Masse-Mensch*, deserves a chapter to itself. I shall write here of two lesser works by Karel Capek, one seen in the Czech National Theater, where it was first produced, the other read in a German translation.

In the first, *The Insect Comedy*, Karel Capek's brother, a scenic artist, has a share as collaborator. It is a fantastic and picturesque piece of satire providing excellent opportunities for the newer methods in production. It is a comment on post-war conditions as symbolized in the life of butterflies, beetles, and ants. The prolog finds a young man wandering in the woods, and puts him comfortably to sleep on a grassy bank after a little talk with an absurdly pedantical entomologist. He sleeps through the three succeeding acts surrounded and occasionally disturbed by figures of insects grown life-size. The first act passes with the brilliant butterflies, who stand for the heedless, unproductive men and women of the social and pseudo-artistic worlds with time for only chatter and flirtation while disaster rumbles beneath them. In the production of this scene, the *régisseur*, K. H. Hilar, keeps the players moving ceaselessly, their hands and heads lightly undulating, with the restlessness of the antennæed world, while high around the back of the scene various of the brightly costumed insects constantly dance behind the translucent curtain of the woods.

In the second scene the humble grubs crawl in and out of their burrows on busy errands of accumulation. These are the assiduous profiteers and misers of war-time society. The act ends in a broad touch of comedy. A beetle has been murdering passing insects and dragging their bodies down below for his wife to hoard. There enters The Parasite, a tramp bug. He does not work. Why should he? He has only to wait for the busy capitalists of his world to fill their larders. Then, when the time comes, he will rise—or more accurately descend—and the wealth of the world will be his. He ducks into the beetle's hole, and in a few moments he comes up, a swollen and jovial Communist, dancing in glee. The everpresent prompter's box serves conveniently for one of the holes, and the background of green and black woods is projected instead of painted; otherwise there is little of interest in the staging of this scene.

The third act carries us to the ants. Here are the eternal laborers, tramping in an endless circle upon their work, under the eye of superiors very like officers and to a rhythm beaten out by a more privileged one of their own number. The Capeks costume the army of ants in khaki, puttees and all, and provide a desolate hill for a background. It might be blasted by either war or commerce. Into its surface descend

35

shafts that might lead to either mines or dugouts. A glowering background of crazy chimneys and telegraph poles and smoke—all projected on the cyclorama—completes the picture. Presently there come shouting and a courier. More couriers. War threatens. The ants drop their burdens for rifles and continue their march. The officer-ants assume a higher station and even loftier phrases of command; from the back they philosophize and give orders in good old Kaiser-fashion. The act culminates with a conflict and the lordship of a new race of ants.

The epilog is divided between the appearance from her chrysalis of an ephemera of whom the sleeping man has been dimly and hopefully conscious in the last two scenes, her death after a dance with other short-lived mayflies, and the despairing end of the human visitor. This end is commented upon in a half satiric and half aspiring vein through the introduction of a group of wanderers who come upon the dead body, gaze at it in astonishment and sadness for a moment, and then pass on, singing, upon the ever-creative way of the peasant.

R. U. R., Karel Capek's other play (in German, *W. U. R.*) is a tale of a Frankenstein such as H. G. Wells might have written in his earlier days. It seems both gruesomely effective and at times philosophic. The letters "R. U. R." are an abbreviation of the name of a firm engaged in manufacturing *"Roboters,"* or workmen stamped out and given life by a machine. After a not very skilful exposition of the nature of this new device for lightening the world's work, the play passes on to show the degenerating effect upon mankind of ceasing to labor. The *"Roboters"* are given pain in order to remind them not to be careless and break their legs and arms. Thereupon they acquire something not unlike a soul. Presently comes a consciousness of their station and their power. They rise and kill all mankind—except one man. Later they find to their dismay that the secret formula of the materials from which they were stamped out has been destroyed. They wear out in twenty years. And there will be an end. The last act shows their frantic appeal for a way to perpetuate themselves. The one man finds it at last when he recognizes love awakening in a male and a female *"Roboter."* The process of mankind will begin once more. Rather the sort of end that Anatole France would have put to the story—Frankenstein turned man.

None of this, of course—either Kaiser or Capek—is Expressionism very far on its way. Some of it is trivial. Some is interesting enough. Much is decadent or uncertain. But it is not difficult to believe that there is something of the future in it. It is a sign. There is a starlike gleam in even the worst of the mire. Vitality, though often a morbid vitality, animates it. When we see Eugene O'Neill saying Nay to Realism in the same fashion, and turning out so strong and significant a play as *The Hairy Ape*—a play that grows greater in the perspective of Europe—it is not very difficult to hope and to look forward.

In the artists who give Expressionism a physical form and a pictorial atmosphere upon the stage we find still more of hope. They have gone more quickly and more securely towards their goal. They have had a disciplinary practice upon the plays of an earlier time, a time before Realism. They are freed from the moral problems of the writer; and where their work is distempered with the morbidity, the unhealthiness, of so much of our time, the result is less obvious in color or design than it would be if it took the form of words. And they have had behind them the history and the example of the movement in art which we once called Post-Impressionism, but which follows logically into Expressionism, the movement of Cézanne, Van Gogh, Matisse, Picasso, Duchamp.

The problem for the expressionist play is the problem of music. And yet not its problem; for music, being so markedly apart from actuality in its materials, has made few and not very successful attempts at the Realism which has swamped our stage. Music has been by very nature expressionistic. It has failed whenever, as program music, it approached the suggestion of the actual. For the rest, it has soared, soared easily, surely, towards direct expression of spiritual reality. Expressionism in the theater has to seek the way of music, the way towards beauty and ecstasy. The difficulty of the playwright is that he must always feel the pull of the actual life about him; he must make his drama out of human beings and not out of pure vision or pure emotional response. The world about him is corrupt and corrupting outwardly, as well as beautiful and wonderful within. He cannot, like the musician, leap away from its entanglements by putting his hands to an instrument of abstract art. But he can gain a certain release by forswearing as much as possible the reproduction of the actual.

CHAPTER IV

BLACK CURTAINS

TO-DAY we are thinking more and more of the future of the theater, the future of the play and the playwright, the future of production, of direction and the actor.

If we are to think of the future to any effect, we must think of the past as well as the present. The path of to-morrow strikes off from the maze of to-day. To guess at its direction with much chance of success, we must look now and then at the map of the settled roads of yesterday.

If we want to estimate the chances of the non-realistic play to advance beyond its expressionist beginnings in Germany, we must try to understand the present state of the art of theatrical production, and the past of play and players, the theater and its stagecraft. A share of the future—a very large share, I believe—may lie with America; but the past is Continental. And a surprising amount of the past is German.

The past of the play shows one interesting peculiarity. The great plays of the romantic movement were developed where there were great theaters, in France and in Germany. Quite

40

otherwise with Realism. Its greatest works—the plays of Ibsen and Strindberg—were created in small countries almost outside the consciousness of the nineteenth century theater. This was natural enough. Realistic plays were, in the last analysis, lonely literary rationalizations. They were not theatrical. They did not spring out of the theater. Instead they altered the theater to suit their needs. The theater that they altered most was the German theater, and there the dramas of the Scandinavians found their best audience.

But the German theater, being a healthy theater, could not stop at the point where it became an almost perfect mechanism for presenting these plays. Its directors and its artists went on experimenting. They had old plays to mount, also, plays out of the romantic and classic periods. They put their brains and their machines at work upon these pieces, as well as upon the realistic, and soon they had developed methods of production for non-realistic plays quite as admirable for the purpose as any of their tricks for lifting the fourth wall before our very eyes. The German theatrical organization became more and more restive under the realistic plays and the old "classics." It was preparing for something new. The *Zeitgeist* was working. Soon it began to work upon the playwrights. There came abortive beginnings in the expressionist plays I have written about in the last chapter. And the German theater went on—and goes on—experimenting.

41

Let us look at this theater a little more closely. For it is the Continental theater to-day as it was yesterday; France has only Copeau, England experiments in little theaters as America experimented ten years ago. And where the Continental theater is, there we are very likely indeed to find the Continental play of the future. The expressionist drama, like every school of drama except the realistic, is a product of the theater in form and vitality, quite as much as it is a product of society in its mind and materials.

The story of the artistic development of the German theater past the realistic stage is familiar enough. It began in 1905, it was fairly complete by 1914. It was founded upon Gordon Craig and Adolphe Appia, and it is symbolized in the name of Max Reinhardt. It made Realism still for Ibsen and Strindberg; but it plowed past the Realism of Otto Brahm—which is the Realism of Belasco—and it achieved a pregnant actuality so direct and simple that it soon gave birth to a new imagination.

The new methods of production are fairly easy to grasp. They rest on a few general principles. The pretenses of the theater had to be successful pretenses. To begin with, certain tricks of the old theater were forsworn, tricks in the main that failed to succeed. Such an obvious pretense as painted perspective had to go. Footlights had to be curbed; for the illumination must be both more natural and more beautiful.

But, beyond these negative things, the directors sought to achieve positive effects for which they had to call into the theater artists of first-rate ability. The business of these artists, whether working on a realistic play or an imaginative one, was to evoke the atmosphere of the piece in setting and in lights. They fell back on three general principles to aid their sense of line and color in visually dramatizing the action. In the first place they simplified the stage picture. They subordinated or eliminated detail. They put as little as possible on the stage that might distract the spectator from the meaning of the general design (which was the meaning of the play), or from the actions and speeches of the characters. Then, by an adroit use of simple materials and forms, they enriched the setting—along the lines of the play—through suggestion. One detail suggested the nature of the whole. The base of a huge column made the audience visualize for itself the size of the building. Half an arch springing off into darkness created the impression of a great vaulted structure. Finally came a synthesis of all the available and appropriate forces of the theater, and of all the qualities of the play; this implying for the director the establishment of a certain apt rhythm in the performance.

This pictorial reform, backed by such direction and acting as the German theater alone was able to supply, and utilizing all manner of mechanical devices for scene-shifting and lighting, has stood to us for some ten years as the so-called new movement in the theater. It has been familiar through the names of Craig and Appia as pioneer theorists, of Reinhardt, and of artists like Ernst Stern and Alfred Roller; through an occasional production from abroad, like Reinhardt's *Sumurûn;* and, at last, through the exceptional work of our own artists in America and the men—from Arthur Hopkins to directors of little theaters—who have given them their opportunities or amplified their conceptions.

Fringing the outside of all this in the past have been bastard minglings of old technique and new spirit, such as Bakst and the Ballets Russes displayed, and the beginnings of theory and experiment leading towards a new—or a very old—sort of theater, a theater cut off from the whole peep-hole convention of the proscenium and the fourth wall.

The strength of this movement in Germany lay partly in a very few talented directors like Reinhardt and artists like Stern, but very greatly in the vigorous and healthy organization of the German theater. Because of the division of Germany in small kingdoms and duchies, there had always been many centers of artistic life, each about a court in the capital. In a score of cities, enriched by industrial development, there were theaters endowed by the state or the city, and directed towards the highest artistic accomplishment. In the larger cities privately owned theaters followed the lead of the public

The Palace: a setting by Hans Strohbach for *Der Traum, ein Leben*, a fantasy by Calderon. Columns of dull gold, painted to suggest a spiral shape, are spaced against a black curtain, which is later drawn aside to reveal a blood-red sky. In the foreground a group of plotting Orientals.

institutions. The strength of these houses lay in their endowment, their ideals, and their system of organization. This was the repertory system. Here, as nowhere in England or America and only here or there in France, were theaters directed by a single mind, employing a permanent company of players, maintaining a repertory of plays, old and new, given in recurring succession night after night, theaters retaining therefore a permanent audience, dependable both in pocketbook and in taste. Supplementing these theaters were organizations of playgoers among the middle and lower classes, such as the Freie Volksbühne in Berlin, which widened the audience of subscribers to good work in the theater. Between endowment and the security of a permanent audience, it was possible for these German theaters to give uncommonly fine performances at uncommonly low prices.

Along with the development of new methods in production went a good deal of activity in theater building. In practice, as well as in theory, Max Littmann and Oskar Kaufmann, following Schinkel and Semper, who had worked with Goethe and Wagner, did much to improve the auditoriums of German theaters. The result is not so marked as in the case of the scenic artists. Most of the theaters are old indeed and awkwardly shaped, and too many of the new ones continue the tradition of a parquet surrounded and surmounted by three or four shallow, horseshoe-shaped balconies. These balconies are not so good to see or hear from as our own. A realization of the awkwardness of these shelves or *Rangen*, as they are termed in German, produced an opposition, headed by Littmann, that called for their elimination and for the substitution of an amphitheater type of house with no balconies and with a steeper floor to allow of better sightlines. The fight of *Ring vs. Rang* has resulted in several auditoriums designed by Littmann, the Prinzregenten Theater and the Künstler, for example, in Munich, the slant of whose floors is far too sharp; from the upper rows, the players are seen as in some far-off pit. The slant is greater than necessary, and absolutely straight; the practice of the American architect, H. C. Ingalls, of grading the floor in a gradually increasing curve, produces a far better effect. A compromise between *Rang* and *Ring* might be found in a development of the American house with only one balcony; a more steeply slanting floor than we ordinarily have would thus bring two amphitheaters or *Rings* into a single auditorium. Germany possesses, however, some admirable playhouses in the Kammerspielhaus formerly directed by Reinhardt in Berlin, in the Volksbühne designed by Oskar Kaufmann, and in many features of the Künstler Theater. The seating arrangements have formed one of the best features of the German houses. The chairs are almost always too thinly padded; but the elimination of aisles more than compensates. The whole audience is united in a single responsive body. And because each row is a little wider than ours and the side walls of the auditoriums are liberally supplied with doors, the audience empties out more quickly than ours and in an orderly manner that puts American fire-regulations to shame. I have seen the three thousand spectators of the Volksbühne walk out in a single minute. It takes from three to four for a small theater in New York, seating only six hundred, to clear itself.

A factor that has done a great deal for the progress of the German theater and the reputation of the new stagecraft, is the liberal attitude of the German periodicals and publishing houses towards new things in the theater. Editors and writers have been so eager to present to the public every smallest reform in setting or theater that the world has gained rather an optimistic view of the extent of production progress in Germany. Just as it is a fact that only in a few theaters will you find model auditoriums in Central Europe, in a similar way you discover that the outstanding work of design before the war was done by two men, Stern and Roller, and that the other men whose names decorate the records of the new stagecraft were each responsible for only a few productions.

One thing further you may learn about the past of the German movement, even in an investigation so late as the summer of 1922. And that is that the color in a great majority of the stage settings has been very far from good. The German has an ear, a very marvelous ear; only the Russian can approach him in music, and it is not a near approach. But his eye is bad. Germany has produced no first-rate artists except Dürer, Schongauer and perhaps Cranach, and Dürer and Schongauer are celebrated as etchers rather than as painters. That should have been caution enough for those of us who had to study the German stage at the distance of the half-tone. The fact of the matter is that the German is a splendid theorist, a man of large conceptions, and that therefore in the theater he has been able to design settings of simple and excellent proportions, which create a good effect in black-and-white. It is his sense of color that is at fault. Stern, with the mixture of the Oriental in his blood which did so much for Bakst, and some of the artists from Vienna and the South brought something to the stage besides dramatic imagination and sense of proportion. The test of color downs the rest.

When we think of the future of the German theater we must naturally think of the present also, and it is a black present. Germany has been shattered spiritually as well as economically. It has fallen from dreams of world-dominion to bankruptcy and enslavement. The effect of this upon the mind of the citizen who has come through four years of danger and privation, is staggering. One incident of the fall, which you learn upon visiting Germany, is sharply significant. Until the soldiers from the broken German armies began to stream back into the Rhine provinces in November, 1918, the men and women behind the front believed that their forces were victorious. It is possible for the theater to go on physically under almost any conditions of privation; but you must reckon spiritually with an extraordinary state of the public mind when you prophesy the future of the German theater. Two things, perhaps, make optimism possible. One: Germany and the German people have gone through terrible things before; there was the Thirty Years War. Two: Germany still has the wonderfully trained audience of pre-war days; it was a broad democratic audience, and no shift in economic circumstances can destroy so large a part of the cultured playgoers as war-poverty has done in England, in France, and even to some extent in America.

War—backed by the movies—has done its worst in the Berlin theater. Here we find another example of the exchange of ideals and personalities which has often been noted between victor and vanquished. Just as America has been Prussianized in its attitude towards the foreigner and the liberal or radical minority, Berlin has adopted many of the most evil features of the American theatrical system. Within three years of the close of hostilities Berlin was being rapidly Broadway-ized. Repertory was practically dead at all but three or four theaters. Facing economic difficulties and the competition of the movies for the services of the actors, Berlin found

49

it was a large enough city to support long runs for exceptionally great or exceptionally mediocre plays. Even the three theaters that Reinhardt formerly directed broke from repertory, and where they had once shown ten or a dozen productions in two weeks, they showed only three or (counting Sunday matinées of some old favorites) four. Outside Berlin, repertory continues in the State and City theaters and even in private ventures; but many artistic playhouses are badly crippled by the economic troubles of the nation, and some are forced to close down.

There are certain good signs. The theaters were full in 1922. In fifty or sixty visits to the theater it was only at musical comedies that I saw more than one row of vacant seats; in all but half a dozen cases every seat was sold and occupied. The prices were not high. In Frankfort, an average city of the larger size, the highest prices ranged from sixty marks (at that time twenty cents) to one hundred and twenty marks, depending on the expensiveness or the popularity of the production; while the lowest prices for seats were twenty marks to seventy marks, with standing room at six marks.

At such prices even full houses do not make budgets easy to balance. The theater of post-war Germany must be economical in its expenditures. That is not, however, such an artistic hardship as much of the talk of elaborate machinery

50

and handsome productions in pre-war days might suggest. Rigorous physical simplicity and a reliance on the genius of design instead of elaboration of mechanics are the vital needs in stage setting to-day. Germany has done fine things in the simplifying of production, and it has done them in spite of the temptations of bulging pocketbooks. What it may be forced to do now through poverty is a matter for real hope.

The danger—for there is a danger—is that smaller minds may find an excuse for a mean sort of simplicity, a bareness and barrenness of spirit. There has always been a tendency among the modern directors and designers to economize spiritually as well as economically. The results have been seen in some of our dry, meager "little theater" productions, full of bare formalism—a sort of "simplism" that has no place in any art, let alone in the live, varied, rich, and vigorous theater. Occasionally a German artist of real talent falls into this thin manner; Ludwig Sievert has mounted *Towards Damascus* at the Frankfort Schauspielhaus upon a scheme which is physically interesting, but he has given his settings a mean, arid, spiritually poverty-stricken appearance which is never beautiful, and does not express in the least the intense quality of Strindberg's play.

The movies break up ensemble in Germany, and bear down on repertory. They offer salaries that the actor, impoverished quite as much as the worker, cannot resist. Moreover they demand from him the daylight hours which must be given to rehearsals of old and new pieces if repertory is to exist. The German actor cannot appear in a repertory theater in the evenings, as our actor can appear upon Broadway, and put in his days in front of the camera, as ours often does. But—and this is highly important—the German actor has been trained in a school of ideals and self-expression which makes him demand more than the movies can give him. He must have some sort of serious work in the theater, and he is finding it more and more in special summer engagements or *Festspiele.* Thus many of the greatest of the nation's players are often assembled at salaries which, by comparison with their motion picture earnings, are hardly salaries at all.

There remains the spirit of the German people. The audiences are intact and intelligent, but what about their spirit? Can these people live down their sufferings or lift them up to something great outside themselves? The prospect is not so dark in the southern parts, in Bavaria, perhaps; it is certainly bright in Austria, where hunger and economic misery are the realest and where the divinity of the human spirit is asserted again and again in every happy gesture of this lovely people. In Berlin it is another matter. Spiritual dejection and gnawing misery are in the face of every one. They are to be seen on the stage, too. Berlin does not go to the theater to be taken out of itself; it seems to neglect the prime use of art.

Berlin demands an echoing misery from its playhouses. It goes to see a blacker and more despicable *Richard III* than Shakespeare ever imagined. It suffers the torments of disillusioned revolution in *Masse-Mensch* at the working people's theater. It throngs the glowering caverns of the Grosses Schauspielhaus. And everywhere the stage is hung in black curtains. "Warum immer die schwarzen Vorhänge?" we ask again and again. Perhaps they are only an accident of the attempt to get a background of emptiness; but they become a yawning gulf of spiritual blackness. The only colors to break the pall are the red of blood, and the blue that strikes across the black a symbol of a sinister cruelty.

Of course, black curtains are no Teuton monopoly. When the Russian Pitoëff uses them in Paris, when we see them on Broadway and in our "little theaters," we do not look for the words "Made in Germany" on the selvage. But in Germany they seem numerous and more significant. If the curtains were sometimes dappled with gray or if they were opalescent with hidden lights, they might be significant of nothing more than the Germans' immensely active experiments with a formal stage. Perhaps *bunte Vorhänge* are coming. Perhaps it is always a little dark before dawn.

CHAPTER V

THE TWILIGHT OF THE MACHINES

THERE are many things upon the German stage besides black dawn. The twilight of the machines, for instance, and all the past of the new stagecraft lagging superfluous.

Even the past of the old stagecraft. In the same theater in Frankfort where one of the three significant pairs of German directors and artists labors, I have seen *Peer Gynt* given as incompetently as any patron of an American small-town stock company could demand. The settings were hideous; the same badly painted backdrop served for two or three scenes in different localities; the revolving stage rumbled noisily and did nothing to shorten intermissions. While the orchestra played Grieg's introductory music in the wings and the stage was dark, waiting actors, who imagined that thereby ears as well as eyes were dimmed, restlessly shifted from one foot to another in squeaky shoes. At the beginning of each scene the lights came up like thunder. Through as many scenes as could be endured, the same players who gave a sharp, almost electric performance of *Maria Stuart* the next night, acted

54

The sleep-walking scene from *Macbeth* as produced by Harald André at the Royal Opera in Stockholm.   Moonlight slants down through four tall windows making alternate bars of light and shadow, through which moves the white-robed figure of Lady Macbeth.   The Doctor and the Gentlewoman are half-hidden at one side in the darkness of the foreground.

Peer Gynt dully and sloppily to a running fire of assistance from the prompter's box. It is worth remarking, incidentally, that the *souffleur*, as he is euphemistically called, is no necessity in the repertory theater. He may give a complete and studied reading of the text one lap ahead of the actors in the Grosses Schauspielhaus, the Frankfort Schauspielhaus, the Burgtheater in Vienna, the Lessing Theater in Berlin, and a dozen other first-class theaters; but you don't hear his voice in the State Schauspielhaus of Berlin under Jessner, in Copeau's Vieux-Colombier in Paris, or during a performance of *Masse-Mensch* at the Volksbühne.

The past of the German stage is seldom slovenly, but it is often disturbing. To see in 1922 a setting by Roller for *Die Meistersinger* is like encountering at a fashionable New York *thé dansant* the girl you used to take to high school dances in St. Louis in 1907. The German stage is full of such disquieting reminders of juvenile infatuations; Sweden is not exempt. The work of the pioneers and imitations of the work of the pioneers are still to be seen. Verdi's *Macbeth à la* Craig at the Stockholm Opera; *The Sunken Bell* at the Grosses Schauspielhaus with Stern's hill from *Penthesilea;* Reinhardt effects in *Maria Stuart* in Frankfort; good old Russian painting in faked perspective in *Florian Geyer* in Munich; a wedding of Heinrich Leffler and Maxfield Parrish at Dresden in the Verdi opera which the Germans so cheerfully translate as

Der Troubadour; the style, if you can call it that, of the Washington Square Players in *Towards Damascus* in Frankfort. Everywhere traces of Reinhardt and Craig and Roller.

Roller, alone of the artists who were new fifteen years ago, is still busy in the theater. The mood he arouses is mixed. It is thoroughly annoying to find him so unable to grasp the problem of setting in the remarkable new theater in the Redoutensaal in Vienna, unable to see that the Gobelins and the crystal, the golden moldings and the rich baroque ornament of that marvelous room which is both stage and auditorium, must set the style and color of the screens and formal set pieces of the stage. It is a little sad to see Roller trying in *Kain* at the Burgtheater to adopt the steps and black curtains and the one or two plastics of the newer and younger men. When he is decking out some war-horse like *Die Meistersinger* in the good old style of the revolutionists of 1910, you have to forgive him much, even while you wonder at the limitations of so many of the stage designers outside Russia. Take the first scene, for example. Dramatically the thing is right in proportion and arrangement. It is an interesting composition of wall spaces and doors, which becomes all the more interesting when the director has arranged the many costumed characters in waves that ripple along the shore of the picture and roll up here and there about some promontory of the design. But when you look away from composition to color, you see a lack.

A setting by Alfred Roller for the first act of
Die Meistersinger at the State Opera in Vienna.
An example of the purely decorative setting at its
best.

It is not the difficulty of bad color, which besets most of the Germans; Roller and Stern generally escape that. The fact of the matter is that there simply isn't any color—in spite of a furnace of dulled orange smoldering on the walls, and some gray-greens damping it down for contrast. This is not color in the sense that the Russians know it. Roller does not think in color as does Nicolas Roerich. What Westerner does—or ever has? Roller thinks in line and mass and proportion. Then he goes to his paint-box, and selects two nicely contrasting tones, more or less appropriate to a large medieval building. He never bothers his head over the dramatic problem of whether they mean anything in relation to the action, or the artistic problem of whether he has made one of those subtle arrangements of many curiously harmonizing colors, which, in the alchemy of the eye, take on a psychic significance.

Such laggard things—the relics of Craig-ideas and the work of various of the elder directors and artists—play a more or less normal part in the life of the German stage. They would find a parallel in any age. They know their place and keep to it. Something that is only just beginning to learn its proper and subordinate part in the advance of the theater is the far-famed stage machinery of Germany.

It was the most natural thing in the world that the Germans should turn their stage into a machine shop. When they build one of their great five-story office buildings they begin by laying a railroad along two sides on the street level and another up in the air above it, and putting in a traveling elevator, dump-cart, and crane that runs along on the tracks; after they have this gigantic apparatus in order, building the building is mere child's play. *Der verrückte Krieg* was all that prevented the development of a most ingenious mechanism for erecting the erector that builds the building.

The German stage machine is a Frankenstein stage-hand. It is intended to do the work of scene shifting at great economy of effort and time. Actually the German theaters seem to employ more stage hands than the American theaters, and the waits are no shorter on the whole than those we are able to manage if we want to.

There are two main divisions to the species. Lewis Carroll, listing the different varieties of Snarks, supplied a formula. There are those, it is said, that are round and revolve, and those that have rollers and slide. The revolving stage—made famous by the cohorts of Reinhardt—and the sliding stage—which includes a sinking variety.

The revolving stage has its furious adherents. They include Reinhardt, Stern, who utilized its shortcomings quite as marvelously as its good points in his productions for Reinhardt, and the host of Reinhardt disciples. It came from Japan in 1896 through Lautenschläger of Munich. It is a great circle cut out of the stage floor and mounted on wheels so that it may be freely turned by hand or power. The circle is from forty to sixty feet across, and usually occupies the greater part of the stage space. On it the different settings are placed back to back, anywhere from two to ten fitting snugly together. One after another of these settings is presented in the opening of the proscenium as the stage revolves. It retains its reputation because it is the simplest and handiest scene-shifting machine to use with the great solid plaster dome which Reinhardt and so many other directors found essential as a substitute for the flapping and wrinkling canvas sky.

The sliding stage pure and simple is just a couple of low platforms the size of that part of the stage usually acted on. These carry the settings and slide out sideways into the wings. While one platform is in front of the proscenium with the actors giving the play in its setting, the other is being reset at the right or the left. It is easy to see that these platforms cannot slide past either end of the plaster dome if it is far enough down front to be of any use. The Deutsches Opernhaus in Charlottenburg, Berlin, gets around this by having the whole gigantic dome slide, too; hung from tracks and carrying its lights with it, the dome is pushed back into the depths of the stage when the platforms at the front have to slide. The amusing feature is that the present director of the theater has so little notion of what it is all for that in *Don Giovanni* he makes a number of changes by rigging his flats and drops on lines, as we might do, and hoisting them into the flies in full view of the audience on what is by a polite fiction called a dark stage.

All this whirling of palaces and scuttling of skies is child's play beside the sinking stage. As developed by Adolf Linnebach, technical director of the State Schauspielhaus in Dresden, it almost defies understanding or description. The simplest variety is to be found across the National Gallery and the Theaterplatz under the guiding and inventive hand of Max Hasait of the State Opera House, Linnebach's great mechanical rival. The stage of the Opera is divided into seven sections from the proscenium opening to the spot a hundred feet back where the *Hinterbühne* or auxiliary rear-stage begins. These seven sections can rise some feet above the stage level or sink into the basement. While the front sections are in the basement, carrying a setting that has already been used, the rear sections, with another setting on them, can, by a complicated arrangement, be rolled down on tracks to take the place of the front sections in the proscenium opening. While the front sections are in the basement the setting upon them is changed; the same thing happens to the rear sections when they are rolled back again. The stage of the Schauspielhaus is far more complicated. It is divided in only three sections, but when the two forward sections are in the basement, sliding stages of the ordinary sort, which rest upon them, can be slid

Der Schatzgräber: the cottage of the epilogue in Schrecker's opera. An extreme conventionalization of the old scenic materials. The artist, Emil Pirchan, has indicated a cottage by the shape of the opening in the flat drop. Here, design replaces machinery in securing a quick change of scene.

out to the sides for changes of scene. On these sliding stages small "wagon stages" or mechanical stage hands operate, carrying large pieces such as stairs and mantels into place. Under the orchestra pit at the front is another contrivance, like a small stage on stilts, which can be trundled onto the first sinking stage straddling the setting. Thus two stages are superimposed, and a sort of elevator stage produced, such as Steele MacKaye once invented. Hasait is nursing a scheme for rearranging his sinking and sliding stages so that the seven stages may run forward, sink to the basement, slide back, rise, and run forward again in rapid succession like an endless chain. The prospect is distinctly startling. Opponents of the new stagecraft have often claimed that the scenery ignores the actor. With the sliding and sinking stage a little further advanced, you can imagine the scenery taking a really furious interest in the actor, pursuing him from floor to basement and back again. You can imagine some new director working out a drama in which a cathedral chases an apostate priest about the stage, or a phallic column pursues the heroine into the darkness of the cellar only to lose her as she rises triumphantly on the last of the seven mystic stages guided and blessed by that unique functionary of the German theater, the *Obermaschineninspektor*.

There are peculiar disadvantages to these expensive mechanisms. The revolving stage simply can't handle certain scenes without ceasing to be a revolving stage. It is impossible to use the entire width or depth of the stage for an exterior without shoving all the other scenes off the "revolver," and giving up its use. All exterior scenes on the revolving stage have to go up over the rooms set at the back. The western prairies and the North German sea coast are equally unpopular with the friends of the revolving stage. The exceptionally fine production of *Masse-Mensch*—with its various great steps the whole width and half the height of the stage, alternating with flat open scenes—received almost no assistance from the "revolver" at the Volksbühne in Berlin. The technical director, putting this stage through its paces and exhibiting such amusing tricks as its ability to rise or sink some six feet at either end, thus producing a slanting floor, confessed that he much preferred some other type of stage.

The sliding and sinking stage has fewer disadvantages; but it is an elaborate, expensive, and cumbersome machine to do the work that designers and stage hands might quite as well accomplish. On the matter of expense, it is disquieting to hear at a scene-rehearsal of *Das Rheingold* that one hundred and fifty men, including electricians, are busy with this labor-saving device. It is still more disturbing to the machine-worshiper to time the intermissions in German theaters, and to find that waits of from two to five minutes are quite as frequent as in America. The explanation, of course, is the costumes. "The stage was all set in half a minute, but we had to wait for the tenor to get into his blue tights." It looks very much as if the *Maschineninspektoren* should have introduced sliding wardrobes or adapted the harnessing devices of firehouses before they put thousands of dollars into sliding stages.

The German technical men are beginning to chafe at the limitations of the machines, to be content to push them into second place. If you talk to Linnebach, at Dresden, once high priest of the sliding stage, you will note with some surprise that the word *einfach* has a Carolinian way of getting into the conversation. Things must be simpler. No big solid sets; instead, some curtains and lights and a dome on which to project painted designs. The word *Podium* also crops out. Like almost all forward-looking artists and directors in Germany, Linnebach wants to put the actor on a sort of tribune thrust out into the audience. He wants to give him back the vital heritage of the Greek and the medieval stages. Linnebach is content mechanically with the devices of the electrician; when he mounted Hasenclever's expressionist drama, *Jenseits*, he made the setting out of light and shadow, a few chairs and tables, only one or two set pieces, and some projected backgrounds.

Machinery like the sinking stage has advantages apart from

63

its ability to change heavy realistic sets. It is difficult to see how the opening scene of Shaw's *Pygmalion*, looking out to the street from under the portico of Covent Garden, could be better created or more quickly shifted than in Linnebach's production. Certainly without the ability to sink with ease the rear part of the stage three or four feet, he could not have given us the natural effect of the street level below the eyes of the audience and the actors. The great virtue of a mechanical stage of this kind is not to shift scenery, so much as to supply economically and quickly different levels for the actors to play upon. The use of levels is one of the important advances of the Continental theater since the war, and the sinking stage helps greatly with this. With a few inner prosceniums and simple backgrounds, it can supply, as it were, an infinite variety of formal stages such as the Continental theater seems slowly to be tending toward.

Barring the realistic and the formal, there is a middle ground in which the machine is of little value compared with the designer. In Linnebach's theater—though not from his designs—a Hindu romance, *Vasantasena*, was mounted frankly and freshly against flat settings in the style of Indian miniatures. This was accomplished, without the aid of stage machinery, by the use of a permanent setting or portal of Indian design, with steps and a platform, on which, framed within an inner proscenium, drops and profiles were changed

Das Rheingold: Alberich's Cave.   A setting by
Linnebach and Pasetti at the National Theater in
Munich.   An atmospheric scene produced by lights
playing across a frankly painted background which
emphasizes the rocky converging lines of a cavern.

much as we would change them. The artist, Otto Hettner, supplied a style, as well as a formal stage, which made the machine taboo. Working with Pasetti at the National Theater in Munich, Linnebach accomplished the changes of *Das Rheingold* quite as easily. In an older production at Dresden, under Hasait, the fields of the gods opposite Valhalla were made of bulky platforms and plastic rocks, which went rolling back behind the cyclorama while up from the basement came in one piece the cave of the Nibelungen with its nooks and corners, its overhanging ceiling, and its whole equipment of plastic canvas rocks, which might have come out of some cavern on a scenic railway. In Munich the simpler levels of the fields in the second scene served in the cave scene also. They were lost in the shadows, along with the side walls, which were hardly more than masking curtains. The rocky cave was suggested wholly by the backdrop. This was painted in broken, converging lines of rock formations. Because of the magic of light, it did not seem like some conventional old backdrop.

The spirit of the theater as it has developed since the war seems to call upon the designer and *régisseur* instead of the mechanician. When artists were building heavy and cumbersome settings, elaborate in physical proportions if not in design, sliding and revolving stages were unquestionably necessary, though we may well ask how much the presence of the

65

mechanisms tempted the artists into such excess. To-day, however, the setting is being stylized, the stage itself made formal. Machinery becomes irrelevant. Copeau does not need it even for the realistic *Les Frères Karamazov;* the Redoutensaal is almost too innocent to suspect its existence. *Régisseurs* of the new sort want something more theatrical than a turntable that any round-house might boast.

The playwright works with the *régisseur* and the artist to this same end. While Dorothy Richardson, Waldo Frank, and James Joyce are busy taking the machinery out of the novel, the playwrights are making machinery unnecessary for drama. They drop "atmosphere," and take up the soul. They seek the subjective instead of the physical. They want to thrill us with the mysteries and clarities of the unconscious, instead of cozening us with photographic detail or romantic color. For all this they need imagination in setting, not actuality. Form carries the spirit up and out. Indications speak to it louder than actualities. Design, which is of the spirit, drives out mechanism, which is of the brain.

The day of the machine is over in the theater, the day of its domination at any rate. For a time it looked as though the name of the old theater in the Tuileries would have to be painted over every stage door in Germany—La Salle des Machines. Now the stage machine is sinking into its proper place—the cellar. A new device is lording it in the theater, but it cannot be called a machine. The electric light is not a mechanical thing. It is miraculously animated by something very like the Life Force, and night by night its living rays are directed to new and unforeseen ends.

CHAPTER VI

LIGHT AS SETTING

IN the 'eighties and the 'nineties, when electricity came into the theater to take the place of gas, light was only illumination. By the first decade of the twentieth century it had become atmosphere. To-day it is taking the place of setting in many Continental theaters. To-morrow it may be part of drama itself.

In 1893 a Swiss doctor named Adolphe Appia published a little book in French on the production of Wagner's music-dramas; six years later he elaborated his ideas in a volume published in a German translation as *Die Musik und die Inscenierung*, the first and perhaps the greatest book of theory on the new art of the theater. Among other things, he discussed lighting at great length. He made a very important observation. He noted that the lighting of the stage of his day was hardly more than mere illumination—something to make all objects equally bright and visible. It was quite as necessary, he believed, to make certain objects more visible than others, and to make them more living, more dramatic. At the time the lighting apparatus of the theater was crude, because the electric light was in its infancy. There were only small electric bulbs, arranged in rows for footlights below and borderlights overhead, to supply flat illumination, and arc lights, which were movable and could be made to "spot" out figures more brilliantly. Appia recognized in these last the means for making the figure of the actor brilliant and dynamic. With his eye on these spotlights he made an unheard-of demand. He asked for shadows. He said that light and shade gave three dimensions to the player and three dimensions to the setting (provided, as he suggested, the setting be made plastic instead of flat). By means of light he wanted to link the living actor and the dead setting. He went further than using shadows and animating the background. He proposed that the play of light throughout an act should express the mood and action. He wanted it to change with the development of the play. He made elaborate analyses of the Wagner music-dramas to show how the light could play a part—an active part—in the setting and the action.

During the next decade, the beginning of the twentieth century, an Italian named Fortuny began the first practical work of progress in stage lighting. Not very permanent work, perhaps, but certainly valuable because it struck out in new directions. His devices have all but disappeared from the German theater; but only because they have been replaced by improvements along the lines he indicated. Fortuny tried to improve the quality of the light by using indirect illumination. He threw light from powerful arcs against colored bands of silk, which reflected it onto the stage. This had two advantages. The light was diffused and broken up. The color could be controlled at a distance by cords that moved the various silk bands past the light. Fortuny also tried to improve the surface on which the light fell. He devised a domed silk sky or *Kuppelhorizont,* into which the greater part of his diffused light was thrown, to be diffused still further. Incidentally he hoped to achieve a better sky-effect. Disadvantages hampered both his devices. Indirect lighting required far more current than direct and created a great deal of heat. The dome was produced by exhausting air from between two curved surfaces of silk, the outer one fastened to a folding frame of steel; creases and joints showed in the silk and air was likely to leak in and collapse the sky.

In the course of another ten years engineering ingenuity supplied substitutes for both these elements of the Fortuny System. Most important was the discovery of how to manufacture incandescent bulbs almost as powerful as arc lights. Such bulbs, equipped with frosted glass and glass mediums or color screens, could not only supply light sufficiently diffused in tone and under easy control, but they also produced the shadows, as well as the light, which Appia wanted. The sky-dome became literally a fixture in the German theater when some one decided to make it out of plaster instead of silk. To-day the high-powered bulb and the plaster sky are everywhere in the German theater. Schwabe in Berlin and Phillips in Holland have succeeded in making bulbs of the enormous power of 3,000 watts or 6,000 candlepower, bulbs about three times as strong as any incandescent lights used in America in 1922. The dome, or some variety of it, is found in practically every German theater. Linnebach estimates that there are twenty true *Kuppelhorizonts*, cupping the whole stage with a curving dome; ten permanent *Rundhorizonts*, plaster cycloramas curving like a great semi-circular wall around the stage; and thirty canvas cycloramas which are quite as large as the *Rundhorizont*, and some of which are so hung as to make a most convenient and efficient substitute for either variety of plaster sky.

The most interesting and significant departures in the use of light on the Continental stage have to do with this substitute for the old backdrop. It began as an imitation of the sky, an attempt to put one more piece of Realism into the theater. It has got to the point now where its really interesting and important uses have nothing whatever to do with realistic fake-heavens. It is being employed as a formal element in a stage design, or else as a surface on which to paint scenery with light.

Perhaps it was economy, perhaps a flash of genius, but it occurred to the Germans that there was no particular necessity of lighting the dome or cyclorama. In these huge stages it

71

stands at least sixty or seventy feet back of the footlights. It is possible, therefore, to make it a dim emptiness by merely turning off the lights that ordinarily shine upon it, or to give it some vague neutral quality from the light upon the stage which is reflected onto the *Horizont*. In *Othello* at the State Schauspielhaus in Berlin, Jessner uses his cyclorama, an ordinary canvas one, as a formal background bounding the space in which his strictly conventionalized indications of settings are placed. Thus it is in some scenes a pale neutral wall, in some a curious violet emptiness, in others a faintly salmon background, in still another a yellow light against which figures move in tiny silhouettes. At the Volksbühne in *Masse-Mensch* the dome becomes a misty void in one of the dream-scenes; and then upon this void move vast, mysterious shadows in circling procession.

Shadows on the dome carry us to a final development of lighting in Germany—the "projection" of scenery, the substitution of light for paint as a means of expression. Many minds have worked and are working on devices to be used for this purpose, but the most important mechanisms find their home in Dresden at the theaters of Linnebach and of Hasait.

As might be expected, Linnebach's is the simpler. He has a dome in his theater, the State Schauspielhaus, and upon this dome or through varnished silk from the back, he throws, by means of a very simple lantern containing an arc light but no lenses, the designs painted on glass. This lantern and the transparent method of projection were used in America with much success by Lee Simonson when the New York Theater Guild mounted Shaw's *Back to Methuselah* in the spring of 1922. Linnebach has made the mountains of *Wilhelm Tell* with projection and the settings of Grabbe's *Kaiser Heinrich VI*, and of the expressionist dramas *Das Bist Du*, *Gas*, and *Jenseits*.

Hasait's simplest method of projection brings you up sharp against the true origins of the thing, and they are almost as old as drama. The puppeteers of old Java had shadow-marionettes centuries before the technical director of the Dresden State Opera made shadow-settings. For Weber's *Oberon* and for Mozart's *Zauberflöte*, Hasait provides a plastic arrangement of inner proscenium and steps, with a translucent curtain at the back. From one side of the curtain he projects a design in shadows by means of a frame hardly two feet wide across which are fastened various thicknesses of gauze. The light that comes through the clearer portions of the gauze is one color, while from a light on the other side of the translucent curtain he stains the shadows with a second color. The hue of both these lights can be changed quickly or slowly as desired, producing harmonies and contrasts of color.

The other devices used by Hasait for projection are embodied in a scheme of stage equipment called the Ars System by the Swedish company that controls the patents for its exploitation abroad. The basis of the system is a canvas cyclo-rama. This cyclorama runs on a semi-circular track hung from the gridiron high above the stage. At one end of the track is a great roller upon which the cyclorama may be wound up, to get it out of the way during an elaborate change of scene. It takes only half a minute for the cyclorama to be run out on the track ready for use. The track itself may be swung downward from its two front corners to permit particu-larly large drops to be hoisted or lowered; but it is wide enough and deep enough not to interfere with the ordinary use of the gridiron. The cyclorama is made of common light canvas, but it is so cut and joined, and hung on a slight slant that it takes up of itself the bulges and wrinkles ordinarily produced in our cycloramas by a change in weather. The invention of this cyclorama is in dispute between those ancient but cour-teous rivals, Hasait and Linnebach.

With this cyclorama goes an elaborate system of lighting manufactured by Schwabe. There are floor lamps, contained in wheeled chariots, to illuminate the bottom of the cyclo-rama. Above the proscenium opening hangs a battery of dif-ferent colored lights—seventy-two in the Stockholm State Opera—which play directly upon the cyclorama, and three high-powered bulbs to light the stage floor. Besides these, the Ars System, as installed at Stockholm, includes three special projection devices also hung above the proscenium, all the adjustments of which are controlled electro-magnetically from the switchboard. One of these is the large cloud-machine, an arrangement of two tiers of eight lamps each, raying out from a common axis. These tiers can move at different speeds and in different directions, while each lamp can be turned up and down and sideways at will. These projectors each house a 6,000 candle-power bulb and hold a photograph or drawing of a cloud. The complex motion of these static clouds when projected on the cyclorama gives an effect of every-varying cloud formations. Almost absolute Realism can thus be obtained. A second and smaller and less flexible cloud-machine with a single central lamp and reflecting mirrors is, for some reason, included in the equipment.

Besides these cloud-machines there is a battery of three high-powered bulbs and lenses, by means of which designs painted on glass slides may be projected after the fashion of a magic lantern upon the cyclorama or any object on the stage. This is the really important feature of the Ars System from an artistic standpoint. Its possibilities are extraordinary. Harald André, chief *régisseur* of the Stockholm Opera, has experimented little as yet with this device, utilizing it only in one ballet. But he has speculated much on the opportunities that it presents for uniting a large group of theaters, similarly equipped, in the exchange of scenic designs for the productions in their repertory. André believes that the economy of projected scenery is important artistically, as well as financially, because it will permit of experiment with many new works at slight expense, and of the rapid reproduction of the successful pieces in many cities at once.

From the absolute, artistic viewpoint of the effect obtained, projection is most satisfactory, though as yet almost undeveloped. Americans who saw the translucent projections of Simonson's designs in *Back to Methuselah* realized how little these drops had the visual disadvantages of the painted variety. They enjoyed a certain incorporeal quality. The landscapes were not defined like huge oil paintings in false perspective. They went into some new category which, for the moment, defeated our analysis. Such projections may in time take on the shallow pretense of painted backdrops, though I am inclined to doubt it.

In the case of the Valhalla of *Das Rheingold*, as projected in Linnebach's production at the National Theater in Munich, the ethereal quality of this kind of "painting" again stands out. The scene is most successful when the lighting is dimmest. In the central portions of the second and fourth scenes, when the stage is fully lighted, the image of Valhalla holds its own against the illumination of the foreground, but the foreground itself fails dismally to match the beauty of the gods' castle. When the plastic foreground is not to be seen, Valhalla hangs in the heavens like one of the shapes of Wilfred's Color Organ,

Das Rheingold: Valhalla. A setting by Linnebach and Pasetti. The gods are grouped in deep shadow on a conventionalized arrangement of rocky levels in the foreground. The castle becomes slowly visible in the sky beyond, built of beams of light, hanging in the air like a great cumulus cloud. At the National Theater, Munich.

a thing that seems to have three dimensions. When the lights upon the stage floor bring out the rocks of the foreground, Valhalla loses the reality of three dimensions. It still seems truer, as well as more beautiful, than the rocks in front. In fact it shows up pitilessly the trivial canvas life of those boulders. But it loses the impression of depth, which it had at first created. This was doubtless a false impression, a foolish illusion.

The projected setting is certainly in another dimension spiritually from those two ordinarily employed in old-fashioned scene painting. It is not in any of the planes of stage-rocks or houses. It does not, however, war with the human figure, curiously enough. It seems likely that the artist or director using projected design must formalize his foreground, as Simonson did, or else hide its commonplace actuality in shadow. Ordinary stage pretenses cannot stand beside the spiritual plastics produced by light.

As for the cloud-machine, so long as it is trying merely to reproduce nature it is utterly unimportant. Something imaginative must be done with it before it can expect serious consideration. In the productions of André at the Stockholm Opera there are at least two hints that the cloud-machine can be used for the purposes of art. One of these, rather poorly managed, is the use of designed clouds instead of natural clouds in one of the scenes of *Samson and Delilah*. The other, not perfectly executed by any means, but most suggestive, occurs in Verdi's *Macbeth*. There in the first scene André sets a wild storm sky in motion. He uses negative or black photographs of clouds instead of positive or white, and he starts them moving from on high and at the sides, sweeping in and down upon the witches. As these dark shapes descend in tumult, it seems as though the black earth were drinking black clouds, curious and evil portent of the powers of the infernal.

Movement in projection has obviously great possibilities as part of the action of new drama. In Kaiser's expressionist play *From Morn to Midnight*, produced by the Theater Guild, Simonson used Linnebach's lantern to make the tree in the snow scene change into a skeleton, an effect that Kaiser was able to foresee only as a shifting of snowflakes upon naked boughs.

Light itself seems destined to assume a larger and larger part in the drama. It is a playing force, quite as much as the actors. It can be a motivator of action as well as an illuminator of it. Jessner at the State Schauspielhaus in Berlin uses it as an arbitrary accompaniment and interpreter of action. Lights flash on or off as some mood changes. They create shadows to dramatize a relation of two men. They seem to control or to be controlled by the action. The extent to which a change of light may express the dramatist's conception is most interestingly suggested in the scene of Macbeth's death in André's production of the opera. It is an uncommonly well handled scene in all respects, perhaps the best example of this director's fine imagination. The fight between the armies begins in a gray light before the walls of Dunsinane. There is no absurd effort of supers to look like death-crazed warriors. The quality of pursuit and conflict is caught in the pose of the bands of the soldiers as they run past the walls bent down like dogs upon a blood-scent. Macbeth and Macduff meet for a clear moment of conflict, then they are surrounded and covered by the troops that rush to see their champions do battle. At the moment when Macbeth falls, the crowd clears for a moment. And then the grayness of morning breaks sharply into dawn as evil goes out of the play. An obvious symbolism, perhaps, but obviousness is not so great a failing in the theater. The fault of the scene is only in André's over-emphasis upon the light, or rather his under-emphasis upon the cause of the light—the death of Macbeth. At the moment when the light goes on, there should come some supreme, arresting gesture, something to absorb every atom of our attention so that we may wonderingly discover the light as a thing caused by Macbeth, not by an electrician.

Such a scene suggests wide possibilities. Light as the compelling force of a play; light as a motivator of action; light and setting, not as a background to action, but as part of it, as something making characters exist and act; light as an almost physical aura of human bodies; light, therefore, in conflict.

Physical contacts are not a necessity of the theater. Under Jessner, the murderer of Clarence in *Richard III* does not try to seem to stab him; he simply plunges the dagger at him. That is enough. In *Francesca da Rimini* as Duse sometimes gave it, I have heard that when the husband killed Paola with his sword the space of the whole room separated them. It was as if the sword possessed an aura, and as if the aura slew. In *Masse-Mensch* the crowd of revolutionaries go down to the mere rattle of machine guns before the curtains are drawn to show the soldiers.

If light can do such things, even if it can do no more than signal the downfall of evil or set Valhalla glowing in the heavens, it will take a place in the theater that no other product of inventive ingenuity can reach. Light, at the very least, is machinery spiritualized.

CHAPTER VII

THE GERMAN ACTOR

FOUR years of war left the elaborate machinery of the German theaters intact. Four years of the purgatory called peace have even seen a sharp advance in electrical equipment. Critics and managers of the victorious nations and of the neutrals that enjoy a sound exchange may complain of the quantity and quality of theater-goers; but the vanquished have suffered less. At forty performances in Germany and Austria we saw hardly two rows of vacant seats all told in the dramatic theaters, though one or two musical shows were no more than two-thirds full.

The German theater has suffered, however, in one spot. The unfortunate truth is that it is a vital spot—acting. Only the richness of trained talent in its post-war companies enables it to suffer the drain of the past years and still give performances far better than we see in England or America.

War affected the German actor less than it did the actor in the allied countries; Germany kept her players on the home front fighting disheartenment. Peace and the movies, however, brought dispersal. Companies were scattered, players exiled.

The spectacular collapse, of course, was the dissolution of Max Reinhardt's famous company that filled his two Berlin theaters. Moissi, Bassermann, Pallenberg, Konstantin, Eibenschütz, Wegener, Dietrich, Arnold, Lehman, Eysoldt, Bertens, Diegelmann, Heims, Jannings, Schildkraut—not one of these names appears on the *Zettel* outside the old Reinhardt houses. Some are in the movies and some are stars, but all are gone.

If American films could have entered Germany in the face of the depreciated mark, Reinhardt's theaters might still be giving true repertory, Reinhardt himself might still be there, and certainly many of the old company would be playing together in Berlin. Other factors, personal, financial, and artistic, gradually drew Reinhardt out of production, but he himself declared with much truth that repertory was impossible when actors had to give their days to the movies, instead of to rehearsals, and that the theater was impossible for him without repertory and actors. As for the players themselves, with the mark at a cent and pomade at two hundred marks, it had to be either the movies or stardom.

The star system of England and America, imported into Germany, has done little to keep even the popular players in Berlin. The audience is exhausted sooner than in New York or London, and then tours must come. Alexander Moissi knocks about Switzerland and Austria. Leopoldine Konstantin, the flashing slave girl of *Sumurûn*, is supposed to be starring in Vienna, but you find her one night at *Der Blaue Vogel*, the imitation *Chauve-Souris* which one of Balieff's assistants installed in Berlin. Pallenberg goes up and down the country with *Der Wauwau*, the German edition of *Grumpy*.

Even the younger stars are wanderers. That fresh exotic, Maria Orska, competes with the traveling troupe of the Moscow Art Theater for the patronage of Stockholm. She plays in the cosmopolitan German of a Russian, against the Swedish of a resident company. The play is Wedekind's *Erdgeist*, first half of that staggering duology of sex which ends with *Pandora's Box* and Jack the Ripper, and goes under the name of *Lulu*. In Berlin Mme. Orska is thought a little sensational. Her Lulu is anything but that. She does not dwell on the corporeality of this daughter of earth's joy. Her Lulu is not a human being made hideous and fascinating with eternal lures. She is a kind of mask, a thin mask, a shell of tinted and whitened silks over a face sucked dry of all but passion and the shrunken charms of decadence. She is a sort of doll—a *Pritzelpuppe*—with her long black legs and her pale face thrust out from either end of a pierrot's costume. Very much of a doll when the play is most bitterly cruel. Dr. Goll flops to the floor, dead, when he finds her with Schwartz. Orska tiptoes stiffly towards him, manœuvers past his body like some marionette, pokes him with a stiff toe and squeaks the squeak of a doll. Is it fear or pleasure or both? A clever way to do Wedekind. But, in the end, night after night with only self-display to remember.

But Berlin—or Stockholm—is not Germany. There is ensemble left in some of the lesser cities—there is even ensemble in Berlin at the State Schauspielhaus, if there is no great individual playing there.

The illustrious old Burgtheater in Vienna still has a company, if it lacks a distinguished director. They manage portions of Tolstoi's *The Living Corpse* very well. They give the episode of the gypsies' singing to Fedya and Mascha as it was never given in our own *Redemption*. In the Burgtheater it is no discreet cabaret turn. The women and the men hang over the lovers. Their song is a frank and touching celebration of the love that their Mascha has won. It is an open display of sentimental interest in love-making, which people only admit when wine or perhaps gypsy blood have stilled inhibitions. But all this is doubtless more a matter of direction than of acting. It is in the old mother of Frau Senders, the aristocrats of Frau Wilbrand and Herr Herterich, not quite so much so in the Fedya of Herr Treszler that you find real playing. It is hardly possible that the performance of Vildrac's *The S.S. Tenacity* is the best that the Burgtheater gives; but it is a most excellent performance. It is peculiarly excellent, because, while it is not French, it seems so little German in a racial sense. Artistically, of course, it is most decidedly Teuton. It has the hard, firm quality of German acting. Copeau's production in Paris is a rational thing; it is almost like a reading, a very intelligent, sensitive reading. In New York we played it in flashes of misgiving and determination; it was unctuous in Augustin Duncan's roustabout and in Claude Cooper's English sailor, and fine and sensitive in Marguerite Forrest's rather ladylike barmaid; but the rest dropped in and out of illusion. The Viennese actors play for a bright and firm actuality, which they imagine is French. It isn't precisely German, but technically it is as Teuton in thorough-going emotionalism as the passionate kiss with which the Viennese players replaced the salute on the nape of the neck with which the French Bastien begins his wooing.

Individual acting as well as ensemble flourishes in the large company that serves the four State theaters of Munich. It is a piece of good fortune that both opera and drama are under a single management, and that pieces may be given in any one of four houses—the small modernist Künstler Theater of Max Littmann in the Ausstellungspark, the tiny, wickedly cheerful old Residenz Theater, the reformist "amphitheater" which Littmann created in the Prinzregenten Theater, or the National Theater, just as much the conventional old-fashioned German opera house as when it was called the Hoftheater. The large company and the breadth of repertory which these theaters permit to be given efficiently and properly, provides some exceptional players exceptionally well-trained and in an interesting variety of parts.

The Munich group can give that shock of virtuosity which the German repertory theaters provide, and give it to you at highest voltage. On one evening, for example, you discover in *The Taming of the Shrew* a most exceptional Grumio. His name is Richard Kellerhals, and he is the sort of clown that happens once in ten years in America. He is not a Charlie Chaplin, because that is a little too much to ask. But he outdoes any other movie-comic that I can recall. He is not a Jim Barton, because he does not drive ahead at just one thing— Gargantuan burlesque. Kellerhals plays Grumio with his face and his legs and his brain. His odd, wizened little face, inordinately simple, just a bit loony; his acrobatic legs, quick and comic, getting him into all manner of strange places; his brain, always alert behind the mask of the loon, working out a dozen amusing twists of business. It seems a highly original performance, though perhaps it is merely tradition in Germany that Grumio should sniff the clothes of Biondello, and be sniffed at, all within the bounds of decency, but very like two dogs of their masters. At any rate, original or not, it is the sort of sharp, brilliant fooling that would make Kellerhals a musical comedy specialist in America, perhaps a star.

An evening or two later, out at the Ausstellungspark you see Hauptmann's play of the Peasants' Rebellion, *Florian Geyer*.

Almost the first figure you notice among the peasants who are trying desperately to make themselves far-seeing leaders in the fight against the trained nobles, is a gaunt fellow with his head in a bloody bandage, and with fever in his eyes. This is Geyer's brother-in-law and secretary in the field, a boy almost on the point of death who looks like a sickened man of thirty. The desperate impatience of the worn is mingled in his face with the fanatical devotion of the men who win lost causes. The cause *is* lost in the end, and after he has watched this disillusion pile upon quarrels and jealousies and treasons, he crumples up and dies. Every word of his tragedy you can read in his face. When you look at your program you find that the name of the actor is Richard Kellerhals. In America—if Kellerhals had acted this part before Grumio—he would be competing with William B. Mack in the playing of tortured gunmen the rest of his life.

Quite as good acting and almost as varied impersonations are to be seen in the work of Friedrich Ulmer as Petruchio and as Geyer. His Geyer—strong, simple, desperate in anger—is easy to imagine on our stage; Lionel Barrymore could do it. But his Petruchio—a coarse, bull-necked, and most amusing devil—is another matter. It sins against the pretty romance of our Van Dyked Shakespeare. And it is famously good fun, along with the whole riotous show.

Dresden has a company that makes no difficulty over playing Shaw's *Pygmalion* one night, in German provincial accents that are supposed to approximate the English dialects pursued and recorded by Professor Higgins under the portico of Covent Garden, and over playing the next night a comic and poetic romance of India called *Vasantasena* by a king called Sudraka. Here the women come out rather more sharply than most of the men, two fine performances in particular by Melitta Leithner as Eliza, the flower girl, and Alice Verden as Vasantasena. The company cannot escape, however, a beefy German tenor-hero, one of the sort that seems in danger any moment of turning into a leading woman with a heavy beard.

Frankfort has perhaps less real acting talent than is to be found in any of the State theaters of the larger cities. It shows an atrocious performance of *Peer Gynt*. Yet, given direction such as Richard Weichert furnishes in Schiller's *Maria Stuart*, and it seems a company of genius. Carl Ebert, a bad Peer Gynt, manages a Leicester of real subtlety; the Elizabeth of Gerda Müller seems a tempestuous horror, and the whole thing is lighted by many excellent small bits of acting.

There seems to be a certain hard, uncompromising insistence in all German acting. It is a thing, perhaps, of narrow spirit and deep intensity. It has unquestioned vitality. In Grabbe's old drama, *Napoleon*, which Jessner gives at the State Schauspielhaus in Berlin, this vitality leaps to union most happily with the intoxication that Bonaparte spread about him always, and never more extraordinarily than in the Hundred Days which this play chronicles. It is all vitality, the impatient vitality of the soldiers of Wolfgang Heinz and Lothar Müthel, who await Napoleon's return, the besotted and sinister vitality of the new mob of the *carmagnole*, the energizing vitality of Rudolf Forster's Wellington, the sober, slow but potent vitality of Arthur Krauszneck's Blücher, and that font of indomitable self-assertion Napoleon himself, played by Ludwig Hartau. Even the old Humpty-Dumpty Louis of Leopold von Ledebur, and the courtiers who prop him up on his throne take on a certain fixity of purpose—perhaps a deathly fixity —from the vitality flowing round them.

In other performances of Jessner's company this vitality flows over into mere vigor, even into violence. That is the besetting sin of the German actor. Fritz Kortner, celebrated for his Richard III and his Othello, ranges from unnatural suppression of feeling, from studied and almost whispered restraint, to mad screechings. An almost neurotic violence crops up somewhere in every other performance in Germany. Even the women fall into it. Gerda Müller's Elizabeth, after an evening of excellent, mastered power, breaks out into the hoarse-voiced raving that seems more a mark of the male players. Sudden spurts of laying it on too thick appear in some of the secondary players of *Florian Geyer*. The comic villain of *Vasantasena* plays the whole thing in a knot of petty passion.

89

It is ranting, this sort of thing, no matter how far it may be from the orotund mouthings of our old-school players, no matter how much sharp characterization and genuine passion may be forced into it.

The performance of *Masse-Mensch* at the Volksbühne in Berlin stands out because it manages to carry intensity of feeling to a point just short of violence, and then, with every excuse provided in this desperate story of thwarted revolution, to bring it up short at the right moment into high-pitched but beautiful vehemence. The outstanding impression must be the astounding diction of the mob that speaks clearly, rhythmically, and most movingly with a single common voice; it gives you a sudden vision of what the Greek chorus may have been, and why thirty thousand people listened. But the power of Mary Dietrich as the Christ-figured, Christ-tortured woman is almost as unforgettable.

Looking back across these forty-odd performances, I find that a very simple and very brief bit of acting stands out as sharply as any. It is the quiet, sadly amusing, little Buddhist priest in *Vasantasena* as played by Erich Ponto. It is not a thing the German stage often discloses, this delicate mingling of humor and reverence. If it were, the people from Moscow who played *The Cherry Orchard* would not have seemed to come from the one land where acting is a rounded and tempered perfection.

CHAPTER VIII

NEW ACTING FOR OLD

ACTING is the oldest thing in the theater. It comes before the play, because in the beginning the actor and the playwright are one. Drama originates when two or three people are seized with a desire to give an old legend or an old ritual a living form. They want to act. As they act they make up their play. The theater becomes the spot that seems a good place—either spiritually, physically, or by force of tradition—in which to give the play. In time comes a division of labor. One of the actors begins to specialize on the play. This actor studies how he can develop the form of the play to make better use of the theater; and then, with some leader among the actors, he begins to speculate on how to change the theater in order to give more scope to the playwright and to the player who interprets him.

That is the history of the theater through twenty-five centuries. It begins with the actor, and it comes very close to ending with him.

It is rather a good thing to understand about the history of the theater. It gives you a certain respect for the actor which actors do not always inspire. It makes you patient with the difficulties of writing anything intelligible on this most ancient and most complex and most unsubstantial of all the things of the theater. It makes you realize the dangers of dogmatizing on the subject. And, if you can look back with imagination to the day of Garrick and his great apron stage and his Hamlet in knickerbockers, back to the day of Burbage and his sunlit platform in the midst of an Elizabethan mob, back to Æschylus answering the chorus of the Furies in the half circle of Athenians that piled up the hillside of the Acropolis; perhaps, then, you will see that the actor was not always a fellow with a false beard or the manners of a soda water clerk, who expects you to believe that he is no actor at all, but a family doctor or an employee of Mr. Liggett who has taken to living in a room with one side gone. At any rate a little hint of theatrical history, full of amazing surprises, might make you tolerant of such speculations as the following on the four types of acting to be seen in the theater to-day and on what is to come of them.

The art of acting is a miscellaneous sort of art. I imagine that types of acting which we think very new and modern were to be found in every age except the first. Probably some famous Greek comedian made his entrance in *The Frogs* looking so amazingly like the statue of Herakles on the Acropolis that for half a minute nobody could be sure that this was really the actor whom they had expected to see. In Shakespeare's day it is not unlikely that the man who played Caliban got together a collection of false hair and wooden tusks which made every one wonder who the new member of the company could be. And probably among the Greeks and the Elizabethans there were players so amazingly like servants or kings in face and carriage that they never played anything else. Yet it is safe to say, nevertheless, that the actor's trick of trying to look like a different human being in each new play and never at all like himself, and his other trick of never looking like anything but himself and always playing exactly the same kind of part, are histrionic symptoms of the disease called Realism. There was never so much literal and deliberate impersonation as in Europe to-day, and so much "type casting" as along Broadway.

These are two very different methods of work, but they both reach the same end—absolute resemblance—and neither has necessarily anything to do with art. The first—for which the word "impersonation" is commonly and very loosely used— is pretty generally esteemed to-day. It is considered to mark off the actor, even the artist, from the crowd of clever mummers. It is hard to deny an instant and hearty interest in any player who can look like and act like a tramp one night, and like a barbaric king the next. The emotion he creates as a king, or the artist's vision he displays in selecting his material and making Form out of it, may be great or small. But his ingenuity in masquerade will always win admiration. In fact we are pretty sure to spend our time praising such an actor as Ben-Ami for looking like a neurotic artist in *Samson and Delilah*, and like a husky young horse-thief in *The Idle Inn*, instead of recognizing the artistic distinction these impersonations show.

Examined in cold blood, the virtue of this sort of acting is the virtue of the wig-maker. The difference between a Van Dyke and a pair of mutton chops; the difference between Flesh Color No. 1 and Flesh Color No. 3; the difference between a waiter's dress suit bought on the Bowery, and a doublet designed by James Reynolds and made by Mme. Freisinger—that is the secret of this kind of acting. Not the whole secret, of course, for the pose of the actor's body, the grace or awkwardness of his carriage, the lift of an eyebrow, or the droop of a lip is quite as important. Such things, however, have no more of art or emotion in them than the tricks of make-up. They can give us recollections of real persons or figures in literature, in painting, or in other plays, about whom we have felt emotion. But it is not until the actor puts Form of his own into this lay figure, by the movement of his body, and the emotion of his voice, that anything approaching art can be said to exist.

Stanislavsky may look like a colonel in *The Three Sisters*,

94

and like a spineless gentleman in *The Cherry Orchard*; but that is not the measure of his art. Stanislavsky might even *be* a colonel on leave who took a fancy to acting, or a spineless gentleman who lost his patrimony and fell back on his university reputation as an amateur actor; and he would still have to prove himself an artist.

There is an amusing similarity and contrast between the two varieties of realistic actors. The first impersonates a different character in every play, and never himself. The second impersonates the same character in every play and always himself. The first impersonates by changing; the second by remaining the same.

Provided that there is a large and varied supply of types— military men, bar-keeps, politicians, artist-neurotics, criminal-neurotics, he-men, she-men, rabbit-men, not to mention all sorts of women—the result on a play should not be so very different whichever system of acting is adopted. If a play-goer were to see only one play, he couldn't detect any difference. If he were to see two, he would be likely to get some added pleasure out of the knowledge that the same people were acting both, and he would probably use up on the business of spying out the tricks of it all a good deal of the energy and attention that he ought to give to the play.

There is one practical difference, however, in these two ways of casting a play. You cannot make a repertory company out of types. In spite of the old jargon about Leading Man, Leading Woman, Juvenile, Old Man, Ingenue, Heavy, Character Man, and so forth, no permanent company giving realistic plays can get along without actors who can achieve some sort of differentiation. Since the German theater and most of the European theater is run on the repertory system, the Continental actor is generally a man adept in masquerade. Because America has no repertory theater, because producers in New York pick new actors out of the apple barrel for every new play, and because almost all the legitimate actors of America make New York their headquarters, the system of casting by type is the natural, workable system for us.

Type acting need not mean that the type the actor plays is absolutely identical with his own personality in private life. It usually isn't. But it does mean that, because of his own personality, his physical and mental equipment, the actor is able to play a very similar type to his own. Two excellent examples of this are Frank Craven and Ernest Truex. In real life they are never Tommy Tucker of *The First Year* or the hero of *Six Cylinder Love*, but on the stage they are never anything else. It is just possible that they could be something else, but they began this way, and this way the managers and the public will probably make them continue.

All of which brings up a single artistic point upon which varied impersonations and the repertory theater defeat type casting. Type casting is apt to tie a man to the kind of part he first acts with any ability, and not the kind he can act best. He may be able to play ten different sorts of characters, and one or two of these may release something in him that permits him to be a true artist in his impersonation. But if he happens to play some other of the ten characters first, and play it reasonably well, our casting system may keep him from ever reaching those characters in which he might excel. For another thing, the constant change of parts in a repertory theater gives an actor practice that he cannot get if he repeats type parts in fewer plays, as he must do in America. Through this practice with varying parts, he may come to add something of artistic significance to his work.

A nice esthetic point arises if you find a type-actor—say Craven—giving an extraordinarily good performance. He is playing himself, we will say; yet within that familiar personality, he is achieving just as interesting emotion as some other actor of a different personality, but possessing the knack of varied impersonation, could achieve; he is even reaching a sense of Form, selecting out of his own personality, experience, and emotion, and combining these into a shape that moves us esthetically—whether to laughter or to tears. Is this art? Would it be art if the actor were Georgie Price imitating Craven, or somebody from the Moscow Art Theater impersonating Craven? Would it be art if Craven played a character so different from himself as the *savant* in *He Who Gets Slapped*, and played it as successfully as he has played Tommy Tucker? Unquestionably the answer to the last question would be Yes. As for the others, there is legitimate room for argument.

This business of varied impersonation *versus* self-impersonation arouses a great deal of dispute. The most interesting feature of the squabble is that usually the opponent of self-impersonation or type-acting points back with mournful pride to some of the great actors of the past like Booth or Forrest. When he does this, he passes clean outside of realistic acting. Moreover, he brings into the argument actors, who, while they played a wide variety of parts, never took the trouble to hide behind the wig-maker or to pretend to be anybody else physically than the great Edwin Booth or the celebrated Edwin Forrest.

To-day we have this same kind of acting, I imagine—and this is the third kind that I want to list—in the work of Sarah Bernhardt, Giovanni Grasso, Margaret Anglin, or Clare Eames. If you started out to list the players who use their own mask frankly for every part, achieving impersonation and emotion by their use of features and voice as instruments, you would find many more names of women than of men; for the actress has far fewer opportunities than the actor to employ the ingenuities of make-up. You would also find, I think, that your

98

list was not so very long, and that it contained the names of most of the players of great distinction from Eleanora Duse to Charlie Chaplin. There is magic in the soul of such players, not in their make-up boxes. They create their impersonations before your eyes, not in their dressing rooms. You may, perhaps, be tempted to say that their art lies in the voice, that the face is a mask. But the face is obviously not a permanent mask; it changes not only from character to character in many subtle ways, but from scene to scene, and emotion to emotion. Also, there is Chaplin, the voiceless; his face speaks. It seems a mask, too, but it is articulate.

Such acting may be given—and usually is given—to the interpretation of realistic drama. It belongs at heart to another thing, to almost another age, past or to come. It achieves the necessary resemblance through the inner truth of its art. But it never submits to submergence. It reaches out towards a kind of acting that we used to have and that we will have again, while it meets the necessities of Realism.

This fourth kind of acting may be called presentational—a word that derives its present use from a distinction set up by Alexander Bakshy in his *The Path of the Russian Stage*. Presentational acting, like presentational production, stands in opposition to representational. The distinction is clear enough in painting, where a piece of work that aims to report an anecdote, or to photograph objects, is representational, and a

99

piece of work striving to show the relation of forms which may or may not be of the everyday world, is presentational. In the theater Bakshy makes a parallel distinction between a scenic background that attempts to represent with canvas and paint actual objects of wood or rock or whatnot, and a background that presents itself frankly as what it is—curtains, for instance, or an architectural wall. The distinction applies to acting as well. A Broadway actor in a bald wig or an actor naturally bald, who is trying to pretend that he is in a room off in Budapest, and who refuses to admit that he knows it is all a sham, and that a thousand people are watching him, is a representational actor, or a realist. An actor who admits that he is an actor, and that he has an audience before him, and that it is his business to charm and move this audience by the brilliance of his art, is a presentational actor. The difference deserves better terms, but they do not yet exist.

It is obvious enough that the first actors were presentational. The Greek men who shouted village gossip from the wains, and made plays of it, were villagers known to every one. The actors in the first dramatic rituals may have worn masks, but they were frankly actors or priests, not the gods and heroes themselves. Roscius was Roscius, Molière was Molière; even the Baconians cannot deny that Shakespeare was Shakespeare when he appeared as old Adam. I would maintain that Garrick and Siddons, Talma and Rachel were frankly actors; did

100

they not see the audience out there under the light of the same chandeliers that lit their stage?

To-day our greatest players reëstablish to some extent the bond with the audience when they abandon any attempt to represent their characters through wigs and make-up, and present their own faces frankly as vehicles of expression. In comedy and in tragedy presentational acting comes out most easily. There is something in really great sorrow—not the emotions of the thwarted defectives of our realistic tragedies —that leaps out to an audience. Hecuba must speak her sorrow to the chorus and over the chorus to the people who have come to the theater for the single purpose of hearing it. There can be no fitting communion with the characters who have caused the tragedy or been stricken by it. The sufferer must carry her cup of sorrow to the gods; they alone can drink of it and make it less. And the great fact of the theater is that the audience are gods. It is a healthy instinct that causes many an actress in a modern tragedy to turn her back on the other characters of the play, and make her lamentation to the audience as though it were a soliloquy or an aside.

There are gods and gods, of course, and it is to Dionysus and Pan that the comedian turns when he shouts his jokes out across the footlights. In fact he takes good care, if he is a wise clown, that the footlights shan't be there to interfere. If he is Al Jolson, he insists on a runway or a little platform that will bring him out over the footlights and into the lap of the audience. If he is a comedian in burlesque like Bobbie Clark, he has the house lights turned up as soon as he begins a comedy scene. He must make contact somehow with his audience. If the fun-maker is Fanny Brice, the method is a little less obvious, and it draws us closer to the sort of presentational acting which will dominate many theaters in the future, the sort of acting that presents an impersonation, and at the same time stands off with the audience, and watches it. If the player is Ruth Draper or Beatrice Herford, you have something that seems to me almost identical with the kind of acting I am trying to define.

I present these four categories of acting for what they are worth. They are frankly two-dimensional. They are divisions in a single plane. Other planes cut across them, and the categories in these planes intersect the ones I have defined. Consider almost any player, and you will find a confusion of methods and results which will need more explanation than I have provided. There is Richard Kellerhals, for instance, the Munich player whose strikingly different work in *The Taming of the Shrew* and *Florian Geyer* I have described. This is not impersonation achieved with make-up. It is a thing of expression, a spiritual thing. Take the actors of the Moscow Art Theater. They use make-up to the last degree, but there is always a spiritual differentiation far more significant than the physical, and there is always a sense of the Form of life more important than either. Harry Lauder has one impersonation —The Saftest of the Family—which is so different from his others in almost every way that for the moment he might be a different player. Here is a presentational actor indulging in the tricks of the realistic impersonator, and showing that, while the fields of realistic impersonation and presentational acting are not absolutely exclusive, at least they are somewhat incongruous or at any rate mutually hampering. Louis Jouvet of the Théâtre du Vieux-Colombier presents an opposite phenomenon when he appears in the realistic drama *Les Frères Karamazov* as the horrific old father, Feodor, and in *Twelfth Night* as Aguecheek. These are absolutely contradictory impersonations. In each case Jouvet completely disguises his own personality. The interesting point is that the physical impersonation which he brings to the Russian play is essentially unrealistic. It is all very carefully designed in costume, make-up, and gesture as a broad and striking expression, but not as a representation, of rough dominance. The red face and the green coat mix in the olive-bronze hat. His hair and his hat, his coat and his elbows flare out in lines of almost comic violence. He is very close to caricature in a thoroughly realistic play. Here is a curious mixture of methods and ends—planes and categories cutting across one another and creating new figures.

Copeau's Vieux-Colombier is to-day the most interesting forcing bed of the new acting in Europe—unless the Kamerny Theater of the Russian expressionists is nourishing more than scenery. Copeau's theater, with its naked stage and almost permanent architectural setting, its lack of proscenium and footlights, and its steps and forestage leading down to the audience, makes unquestionably for presentational acting. The illusion of Realism and representation is extremely difficult to attain. In four plays, *Les Frères Karamazov, Twelfth Night, The S. S. Tenacity,* and *Le Carrosse du St.-Sacrement,* varied as they are, we see no great amount of the sort of masquerading which Jouvet does so well in the first two. In the main, the actors keep their own normal appearance throughout; but they are not, of course, playing types. To some extent, therefore, they are working in the vein of Bernhardt and Grasso, striving for impersonation in emotion rather than in physique. Except for a gouty foot and a simple change in costume, Copeau's Peruvian governor in the comedy *Le Carrosse du St.-Sacrement,* and his impersonation of the intellectual brother of the house of Karamazov are outwardly very much alike. It is in the mood alone that he registers the difference. In both, but particularly in the comic governor, there is a touch of the presentational attitude which fills the rest of the company in varying degrees and informs most of *Twelfth Night.* The difference between this acting and what we are accustomed to, is particularly plain in a comparison of the English sailor as played in the New York production of *The S. S. Tenacity*, and in the Paris production—the oily reality of Claude Cooper's impersonation against the rather brash, certainly very dry version of Robert Allard. Allard's performance has the stamp of almost all the acting at the Vieux-Colombier. It is something intellectually settled upon as an expression of an emotion, and then conveyed to the audience almost as if read and explained. In the school of Copeau, who was once journalist and critic, there is ever something of the expounder. It is a reading, an explanation, in the terms of a theatrical performance. It is, to a certain degree, presentational, because in every reading, in every explanation, there must be an awareness of the existence of the audience.

CHAPTER IX

THE REINHARDT TRADITION

PLAYS of a new expressionist quality—profound, grave, ecstatic, and as far from the neurotic as from the realistic—may be written in the next few years without the stimulus of a great expressionist theater or a great expressionist director. How they are going to get themselves properly produced is another matter. They may be conceived out of the spirit of the time, under the stimulus of the expressionist settings of the scene designers; but the *accouchement* will demand a rather expert midwife.

Expressionist acting, on the contrary, will never achieve more than a hint of existence without a director to call it forth. A Copeau is necessary to bring out the freshness of the company of the Vieux-Colombier, and the hints it gives of the new acting. A rather extraordinary director will be needed to banish representational acting, and to put in its place a presentational ensemble, and to fuse it with the new play.

Is there such a man in Europe to-day? Is there already an indication of his coming in the modifications that other men have wrought in acting, in setting, and even in theater?

106

THE REINHARDT TRADITION

We may as well begin with Reinhardt. He has been the greatest man of the theater of this century. He fled from his Berlin theaters in 1920, to find in Salzburg a retreat from disillusion and a place of new beginnings. We found him there in the summer of 1922 preparing to issue forth from the baroque beauty of the loveliest palace of this lovely city to the conquest of America, and to an experiment in Vienna which may make him again the one figure of the theater—the director we seek. And here and there about Europe we came on spasmodic signs of his continued activity—extraordinary plans for a *Festspielhaus* in Salzburg or in Geneva, and productions of *Orpheus in the Underworld* and Strindberg's *The Dream Play* in Stockholm.

It would be better, perhaps, to call *Orpheus* and *The Dream Play* efficient pot-boilers, and to let them go at that. They give no true measure of the man whose strength and vision grew from art-cabarets to which Balieff owes the inspiration for his *Chauve-Souris*, and naturalistic beginnings with Gorky and Wedekind, until he had assembled the most striking company and repertory west of Moscow, and centered about himself the whole theatrical movement which Craig and Appia began. The Swedish productions are worth a moment's attention only, for they show some of Reinhardt's faults, and hint at a virtue.

I write of *Orpheus* alone, because the qualities of the Strindberg drama were only to be guessed at from photographs and reports, all uniting in dispraise. There were lovely things in this performance of Offenbach's operetta for which neither director nor composer could claim credit—the light, clear, nightingale voices of the women of the Swedish Opera, their superb figures, and the icy beauty of blue eyes and ashen hair. But the things I remember from *Orpheus* in which Reinhardt had a share are often disappointing things, scenes slighted, episodes badly lit, above all carelessness of detail. It has been Reinhardt's major fault, this failure to bring every feature of a production to the highest point of perfection within his grasp. He has always been satisfied to slight one part if the whole could be "put over" by emphasis on another part. Those who remember *Sumurûn* will recall things in this brilliantly exciting pantomime that struck them as impossibly slack—bad painting on the canvas flats, a bald contrast between the flimsy front scenes and the solid structure of the court of the harem behind.

In *Orpheus* his negligence seems to have begun in the choice of a designer. A Dane, Max Rée, makes a mess of the scene on Olympus, and gets to nothing better elsewhere than a golden gate from a chapel in Nancy set against a blue night; Cupid against a gray sky, and, for the descent into Hades, white rays from out a great cloud, down one of which the company dances against the velvet black of the back drop. Before now, Reinhardt has let himself wander from his first instincts and desires

The Cathedral Scene from *Faust*. A Reinhardt production of 1912, designed by Ernst Stern. Two huge columns tower up against black emptiness. Crimson light from the unseen altar at one side streams on the congregation and throws quivering shadows of a cross on the nearer column.

—which are usually the instincts of Ernst Stern, his notable designer; there are the horrors of Poelzig's decoration of the Grosses Schauspielhaus to testify to this.

The three moments of *Orpheus* which electrified Swedish audiences are common enough in conception, but they have something of the simple directness and smash which characterized Reinhardt's earlier work. The three episodes are closely linked and make the climax of the piece. There again you can see Reinhardt's method—the expenditure of so much of his care and energy upon the most important action of the play. In *Orpheus* the place for such emphasis is the revolt on Mt. Olympus, and the descent of Jupiter and the gods to Hades. Reinhardt begins with the *carmagnole* of the revolutionists, with their red banners upon long poles rioting about in the light blue of the celestial regions. For the beginning of the descent into Hades, Reinhardt sees to it that there shall be a high point at the very back of the stage, and from here, clear down to the footlights and over them on a runway beside the boxes, he sends his gods and goddesses cakewalking two at a time down into the depths of the orchestra pit. After a very brief darkness, while the cloud and its rays of light are installed down stage, Reinhardt sets the gods prancing down this white and black path into the flaming silk mouth of hell. By recognizing an opportunity for an effect at the crucial point of the piece, and concentrating upon it whatever energies he has for

109

Orpheus, he makes the descent of the gods far more memorable than it can have been in any other production. Yet it all seems a trivial and half-hearted effort for the man who made Shakespeare so tremendously vital at the Deutsches Theater, and lifted Sophocles' *Œdipus* into crashing popularity at the Circus Schumann.

In his day Reinhardt was all things to all men. He began with the great naturalist director Brahm of the Freie Volksbühne. He made a *Night Lodging* of utter Realism. He put on *A Midsummer Night's Dream* in a forest of *papiermâché*. He brought an austere symbolic quality to *Hamlet,* closing the play with those tall, tall spears that shepherded the body of the Dane upon its shield. He made the story of Sister Beatrice into a gigantic and glorious spectacle in *The Miracle.* He championed intimacy in the theater, took the actor out upon a runway over the heads of the audience in *Sumurûn* and finally, at the Grosses Schauspielhaus, he put the spectators half around the players, and thrust the players in among the spectators in the last scene of Rolland's *Danton.*

Instinct led him to the heart of plays, as it led him from Realism and the proscenium frame back to the Greek orchestra and the actor as a theatrical figure. He grasped the emotional heart of a drama with almost unerring judgment, and he bent a tremendous energy to the task of making the heart of the audience beat with it. Occasionally he ignored or could not animate some secondary but important phase of a play. In *The Merchant of Venice*, though he made Shylock rightly the center of the play and built up a court scene of intolerable excitement, his Portia and his Nerissa were tawdry figures. But his successes were far greater and far more significant than his failures. *Romeo and Juliet* he made into a thing of youthful passion that was almost too deep, too intimate for the eyes of strangers. *Hamlet* with Moissi was an experience of life itself, asserting again the emotional quality of Reinhardt as against the esthetic quality of Craig.

It is hardly necessary to speak of the part that Reinhardt played in establishing the vogue of the designer in the theater, of his attempt to bring Craig to his stage, of his experiments with stage machinery and lighting equipment, or of the extraordinary personal energy which made so much work possible. The German theater testifies continually to his influence. Dozens of younger men must be working in his vein to-day. As far north as Gothenburg, the commerical city of Sweden, and as far south as Vienna his influence spreads.

In Gothenburg works a young director, Per Lindberg, who is as patently a disciple as he was once a student of Reinhardt. There in the Lorensberg Theater is the revolving stage, with settings by a young Swede, Knut Ström, which might have been seen at the Deutsches Theater ten years ago. A large repertory brings forth scenery often in the heavily simplified

111

fashion of ten years ago, but sometimes fresh and ambitious. *Romeo and Juliet* appears against scenes like early Italian paintings, with one permanent background of hill and cypresses and a number of naïve arrangements of arched arcades from some Fra Angelico. The artist turns *régisseur* also in *Everyman*, and manages a performance fresh in its arrangement of setting, platforms, and steps, if a little reminiscent in costumes and poses and movements.

In Richard Weichert, of the State Schauspielhaus in Frankfort, you find a *régisseur* who suggests the influence of Reinhardt without losing distinction as one of the three really significant directors of Germany to-day. It is not so much an influence in an imitative sense, as a resemblance in effectiveness along rather similar lines.

Weichert, like so many of the outstanding directors of Germany, has a single artist with whom he works on terms of the closest coöperation—Ludwig Sievert. It is a little hard, therefore, to divide the credit in *Maria Stuart* for many of the dramatic effects of people against settings and in light. You might put down the scenic ideas wholly to Sievert, since Weichert has permitted the use of a particularly poor setting for the scene of Queen Mary's tirade against Elizabeth; a setting which is a sloppy attempt at lyricism in keeping with Mary's speech at the beginning of the scene, but quite out of touch with the dramatic end. If Weichert could dictate the

Maria Stuart: the throne-room at Westminster. Tall screens of blue and gold are ranged behind a dais surmounted by a high, pointed throne of dull gold. At either side curtains of silvery blue. Queen Elizabeth wears a gown of gleaming gold. A Weichert production in Frankfort designed by Sievert.

fine prison scene reproduced in this book, he would hardly allow
Sievert to include the greenery-yallery exterior to which I
have taken exception. On the other hand, can it be only an
accidental use that Weichert makes of the curtains in the
throne room scene? The act begins with a curious arrangement of square blue columns in an angle of which the throne
is set. When the audience is over, pages draw blue curtains
from each side of the proscenium diagonally backward to the
columns by the throne. This cuts down the room to terms of
intimacy for the council scene. The point at which Weichert
must enter definitely as *régisseur* comes when Elizabeth steps
to one side of the room away from her group of councilors
to read some document; then the down-stage edge of the curtain at the side by the councilors is drawn back far enough for
a flood of amber light to strike across in front of the men, and
catch the white figure of the queen. Here in this light she
dominates the room; and Leicester, when he steps into it for
a scene with Mortimer, does the same. It is a device of great
use to the actor in building up the power and atmosphere of
the moment.

The dramatic vigor of Weichert never goes so high in *Maria
Stuart* as Reinhardt's, but he is never so careless of detail or of
subordinate scenes. Almost every inch of the play seems pains-
takingly perfected. Not only are the actors who give so sloppy
a performance in *Peer Gynt* under another director, strung up

constantly to their best effort; but every detail, from contrasts in costuming and the arrangement of costumed figures, to the motion of hands and bodies, seems calculated to heighten the play's emotion. Take the first scene, for example, the prison in which Queen Mary is confined with her few retainers. The drawing shows the interesting arrangement of the scene with bars to indicate a prison but not to obstruct action. It pictures the final scene in a later act, when the queen receives her friends and says good-by before going to her death. The contrast of the queen in white and the others in black is excellent. In the first act, even the queen is in black; the only note of color, a deep red, is given to the heroic boy, Mortimer, who is to bring something like hope to Mary. The long scene between Mortimer and the queen is handled with great dignity, and at the same time intensity. It is studied out to the last details. The hands alone are worth all your attention.

Weichert's direction passes on from atmosphere and movement to the expression that the players themselves give of their characters. It is here perhaps that the resemblance to Reinhardt is closest. You catch it in many places: the contrast between Mortimer's tense young fervor, and the masterful, playacting nonchalance of Leicester; this red and green horror of an Elizabeth, looking somehow as bald beneath her wig as history says she was, and bursting with pent energies and passions; towards the end of the play, Leicester, the deliberate

114

Maria Stuart: a room in the castle where Queen Mary is imprisoned. High black grills fill the proscenium arch on either side. Behind, a flat wall of silvery gray. The sketch shows the moment when Mary, gowned and veiled in white, bids farewell to her attendants. A Weichert production in Frankfort designed by Sievert.

fop, leaning against the wall like some wilted violet, Mortimer exhausted but still strong beside him; then the death of the boy, the quick stabbing, and the spears of the soldiers raying towards his body on the floor. It is all sharp, firm, poised—and very, very careful.

This is the past of Reinhardt—continued into the present and the future by other men. What of his own continuation of it? Some have thought him finished. Fifteen, twenty years of such accomplishment in the theater are likely to drain any man. And indeed Reinhardt does seem to have run through his work in Berlin, and finished with it. No one will know just how much was personal, how much professional, how much philosophic, in the force that drove him to give up the leadership of his great organization, and see it destroyed. The difficulties of management, with increasing costs and actors lost to the movies, undoubtedly weighed heavily. But it is certain that he felt the failure of his big, pet venture, the Grosses Schauspielhaus. It was to have been the crown of his efforts and beliefs—the "theater of the five thousand," as he had called it from the days when he astounded the world with *Œdipus*. In structure and design it was badly handled; it proved a bastard thing and won the severe condemnation of the critics. Added to this was a desire, unquestionably, to shake loose, to get a fresh prospect on the theater, to strike out again if possible towards a final, sure goal. Germans

115

spoke of Reinhardt as vacillating and uncertain in his first years in Salzburg. But is anything but uncertainty to be expected when a man has given up a long line of effort, and is seeking a new one? It is a virtue then to be unsure, to be testing and trying the mind, to be seeking some sort of truth and repeatedly rejecting error.

Certainty began to creep in with Reinhardt's plan for a *Festspielhaus* in Salzburg—a Grosses Schauspielhaus of simpler and more conservative pattern built truer on a knowledge of the mistakes of the first. It was to unite Reinhardt, Richard Strauss, the composer, and Hugo von Hofmannsthal, the playwright. It reached some sort of tentative plan at the hands of Poelzig, who mis-designed the Grosses Schauspielhaus, and Adolf Linnebach, then passed on to Max Hasait, who laid out a stage scheme for some new architect to build his plans around. This scheme called for a semi-circular forestage, with a revolving stage in its center, a traveling cyclorama of the Ars pattern behind this revolving stage, a larger cyclorama taking in still a deeper stage, and another and a larger cyclorama behind that. The proscenium was to be narrowed or widened to suit the size of production and cyclorama. The house itself was to be as adjustable, with a ceiling that let down in such a way as to cut the seating capacity from three or four thousand to fifteen hundred.

While this project waited on capital, an almost hopeless

condition in Austria, and hints began to come that the *Festspiel-haus* would have to be built in Geneva instead, a new opportunity came to Reinhardt's hands through President Vetter, head of the Austrian State theaters, an opportunity of working in a playhouse that agreed with much that Reinhardt had felt about the relations of audience and actor. He was invited to produce five or six plays in the fall of 1922 in the new theater in the Redoutensaal in Vienna. Here, upon a stage practically without setting, and within a room that holds actors and audience in a matrix of baroque richness, Reinhardt will have produced, by the time this book appears, the following plays: *Turandot*, Gozzi's Italian comedy, *Clavigor* and *Stella* by Goethe, Molière's *Le Misanthrope*, and *Dame Cobalt* by Calderon. Here he will have to work in an absolutely non-realistic vein, he will have to explore to the fullest the possibilities of the new and curious sort of acting which I have called presentational. This adventure in Maria Theresa's ballroom will measure Reinhardt against the future.

CHAPTER X

THE ARTIST AS DIRECTOR

THE director of the future may not be a director of to-day. He may not be a director at all. He may be one of those artists whose appearance has been such a distinctive and interesting phenomenon of the twentieth century theater. While we examine Max Reinhardt to discover if he is likely to be the flux which will fuse the expressionist play and the presentational actor, it may be that the man we seek is his former designer of settings, Ernst Stern.

The relation of artist and director in the modern theater has been a curious one, quite as intimate as that of pilot-fish and shark, and not so dissimilar. Attached to the shark, the pilot-fish has his way through life made easy and secure; he is carried comfortably from one hunting ground to another. Often, however, when the time comes to find food, it is the pilot-fish that seeks out the provender, and prepares the ground, as it were, for the attack of the shark. Then they both feast, and the pilot-fish resumes his subordinate position.

We may shift the figure to pleasanter ground by grace of Samuel Butler, the Erewhonian. This brilliant, odd old

118

gentleman, a bit of a scientist as well as a literary man, had a passion for transferring the terms and conceptions of biology to machinery and to man's social relationships. Departing from the crustaceans, which grow new legs or tails as fast as the old are cut off, he said:

"What . . . can be more distinct from a man than his banker or his solicitor? Yet these are commonly so much parts of him that he can no more cut them off and grow new ones than he can grow new legs or arms; neither must he wound his solicitor; a wound in the solicitor is a very serious thing. As for his bank,—failure of his bank's action may be as fatal to a man as failure of his heart. . . . We can, indeed, grow butchers, bakers, and greengrocers, almost *ad libitum*, but these are low developments and correspond to skin, hair, or finger nails."

I do not know whether it would be right to say that directors have grown artists with great assiduity in the past twenty years, or that the greatest of the directors have become as closely associated with particular artists as a well-to-do Englishman is with his banker or his solicitor. At any rate the name of Reinhardt is intimately associated with the name of Stern; Jessner has his Pirchan, Fehling his Strohbach; I have spoken of the close relationship of Weichert and Sievert, and I could point out similar identifications in America. An artist of a certain type has come into a very definite, creative con-

119

nection with the art of production, and he has usually brought his contribution to the theater of a particular director.

The designer is a modern product. He was unknown to Molière or Shakespeare; the tailor was their only artist. Except for incidental music, costume is the one field in which another talent than that of actor or director invaded the theater from Greek days until the last years of the seventeenth century. There were designers of scenery in the Renaissance, but they kept to the court masques. Inigo Jones would have been as astonished and as shocked as Shakespeare if anybody had suggested that he try to work upon the stage of the Globe Theater. The advent of Italian opera—a development easy to trace from the court masques—and the building of elaborate theaters to house its scenery, brought the painter upon the stage. The names of the flamboyant brothers Galli-Bibiena are the first great names to be met with in the annals of scene painting. And they were the last great names until Schinkel, the German architect, began in the early nineteenth century to seek a way of ridding the stage of the dull devices of the current scene painters. Scenery was not an invention of Realism; it was a much older thing. I doubt if any one more talented than a good carpenter or an interior decorator was needed to achieve the actuality which the realists demanded. When artists of distinction, or designers with a flair for the theater appeared at the stage door, it was because they saw

120

The Desert: a setting by Isaac Grünewald from
the opera, *Samson and Delilah*. A vista of hills
and sky, painted and lit in tones of burning orange,
is broken at either side by high, leaning walls of
harsh gray rock. The director, Harald André, has
grouped his players so as to continue the triangular
form of the opening through which they are seen.
At the Royal Opera in Stockholm.

Shakespeare or Goethe, von Hofmannsthal or Maeterlinck
sending in their cards to Irving or Reinhardt or Stanislavsky.

Now what are the relations that this modern phenomenon
has established with the theater through the medium of the
director? Ordinarily they differ very much from the attitude
that existed between the old-fashioned scenic artist and the
director, and the attitude that still exists in the case of most
scenic studios. This is the relation of shopkeeper and buyer.
The director orders so many settings from the studio. Perhaps
he specifies that they are to be arranged in this or that fashion,
though usually, if the director hasn't the intelligence to employ
a thoroughly creative designer, he hasn't the interest to care
what the setting is like so long as it has enough doors and windows to satisfy the dramatist. Occasionally you find a keen,
modern director who, for one reason or another, has to employ
an artist of inferior quality. Then it is the director's ideas and
conceptions and even his rough sketches and plans that are executed, not the artist's. In Stockholm, for example, Harald André so dominates the official scene painter of the Opera
that the settings for *Macbeth* are largely André's in design
though they are Thorolf Jansson's in execution. Even in the
case of the exceptionally talented artist, Isaac Grünewald, with
whom André associated himself for the production of *Samson
and Delilah*, the director's ideas could dominate in certain
scenes. For example, in the beautiful and effective episode of

121

the Jews in the desert which André injected into the first act—a scene for which the director required a symbolic picture of the fall of the walls of Philistia to accompany the orchestral music which he used for this interlude. The brilliance with which Grünewald executed the conception may be judged from the accompanying illustration.

The commonest relationship of the director and the designer has been coöperative. The artist has brought a scheme of production to the director as often, perhaps, as the director has brought such a scheme to the artist. The director has then criticized, revised, even amplified the artist's designs, and has brought them to realization on the stage. And the artist and the director, arranging lights at the final rehearsals, have come to a last coöperation which may be more important to the play than any that has gone before.

You find, however, constant evidence of the artist running ahead of the director in the creation of details of production which have a large bearing on the action as well as on the atmosphere of the play. Grünewald brought a setting to the mill scene in *Samson and Delilah* which was not only strikingly original and dramatic, but which forced the direction into a single course. The usual arrangement is the flat millstone with a long pole, against which Samson pushes, treading out a large circle as the stone revolves. The actor is always more or less visible, and there is no particular impression of a cruel

Samson and Delilah: the mill. A remarkable example of an essentially ornamental theatrical setting, designed by Isaac Grünewald for the Royal Opera in Stockholm. Black emptiness. A slanting shaft of light strikes the millstone in a vivid crescent. As the wheel travels in its track this crescent widens to a disk of blinding light, and then shrinks again. The actual forms of this setting are sublimated into an arresting composition of shifting abstract shapes of light.

machine dominating a human being. Grünewald changed all this by using a primitive type of vertical millstone. The sketch shows the stage in darkness except for one shaft of light striking sideways across. The great wheel is set well down front within a low circular wall. Along the wall Samson walks, pushing against a short pole that sticks out from the center of one face of the high narrow millstone. As he pushes, the stone swings about and also revolves. This allows the beam of light to catch first a thin crescent at the top of the curving edge of the wheel, then a wider and wider curve, until suddenly, as Samson comes into view, the light brings out the flat face of the wheel like a full moon. Against this the actor is outlined for his *aria*. Then, while the orchestra plays, he pushes the wheel once more around. This arrangement is extraordinarily fine as a living picture and as an expression of the mood of the scene. Moreover, it is a triumph for the artist, because it is an idea in direction as well as setting. It dictates the movement of the player and manages it in the best possible way. No other action for Samson is possible in this set, and no other action could be so appropriate and effective.

Examples of similar dictation by the artist—though none so striking—come to mind. In Frankfort Sievert arranged the settings for Strindberg's *Towards Damascus* in a way that contributed dramatic significance to the movement of the players.

123

The piece is in seventeen scenes; it proceeds through eight different settings to reach the ninth, a church, and from the ninth the hero passes back through the eight in reverse order until he arrives at the spot where the action began. Sievert saw an opportunity to use the revolving stage, as well as elements of design, in a way interpreting and unifying the play. He placed all nine scenes on the "revolver," and he made the acting floor of each successive setting a little higher than the last. This results in rather narrow rooms and a sea shore bounded by formal yellow walls, but it permits an obvious unity, it shows visually the path that the hero has to follow, and it symbolizes his progress as a steady upward movement towards the church.

The artist dictating a particular kind of direction is obvious enough in *Chout* (*Le Bouffon*), the fantastic comic ballet by Prokofieff which Gontcharova designed for the Ballets Russes. Gontcharova's settings are not particularly good, but at least they have a definite and individual character. They are expressionist after a fashion related more or less to Cubism. They present Russian scenes in wildly distorted perspective. Log houses and wooden fences shatter the backdrop in a war of serried timbers. A table is painted on a wing, the top tipping up at an alarming angle, one plate drawn securely upon it, and another, of *papier-mâché*, pinned to it. All this sort of thing enjoined upon the *régisseur* a kind of direction quite

124

The first scene of Tchehoff's *Uncle Vanya*. Here
Pitoëff indicates a Russian country side by a rustic
bench and slender birch trees formally spaced
against a flat gray curtain.

as bizarre, mannered, and comic. *Chout* seems to have had no direction at all in any creative sense. The *régisseur* failed to meet the challenge of the artist.

It is ordinarily very hard to say what share the artist or the director has had in the scheme of a setting, or whether the director has bothered his head at all about the setting after confiding it to what he considers competent hands. It is an interesting speculation just how much the physical shape of Reinhardt's productions has been the sole creation of his artist, Stern. Certainly Stern delighted in the problems which the use of the revolving stage presented, and only in a single mind could the complexities of these sets, nesting together like some cut-out puzzle, be organized to a definite end. It is entirely possible that, except for a conference on the general tone of the production, and criticisms of the scheme devised by Stern, Reinhardt may have given no thought at all to the scenery. Stern was a master in his own line, and for Rinehardt there was always the thing he delighted most in, the emotional mood produced by the voices and movements of the actors. His carelessness of detail even in the acting, suggests that for him there were only the biggest moments, the important elements and climaxes, that put over the emotion of the play.

Sometimes artist and director are the same, as with Pitoëff in Geneva and Paris, or with Knut Ström in Gothenburg. In such a case setting, direction, and acting are one. But ordi-

125

narily there is a division of responsibility, and an opportunity for the artist to play a part in the production of a drama far more important than Bibiena's. Just how important it may prove to be is bound up, I think, with the future of the theater as a physical thing, and with the temperament of the artist. Working as a designer of picture-settings, the artist can only suggest action, but not dictate it, through the shapes and atmospheres he creates. The important thing is that almost all the designers of real distinction in Europe are tending steadily away from the picture-setting. They are constantly at work upon plans for breaking down the proscenium-frame type of production, and for reaching a simple platform stage or podium upon which the actor shall present himself frankly as an actor. This means, curiously enough, that the designers of scenery are trying to eliminate scenery, to abolish their vocation. And this in turn should indicate that the artist has his eye on something else besides being an artist.

The director who works in such a new theater as the artists desire—in the Redoutensaal in Vienna, for example,—requires an artist to work with him who sees art in terms of the arrangement of action upon steps, and against properties or screens. This is ordinarily the business of the director in our picture-frame theater; with the work of the artist enchantingly visible in the setting behind the actors, the director can get away reasonably well with the esthetic problems of the relations of

A scene from Grabbe's *Napoleon*. The Place de
Grêve in Paris is indicated by a great street lamp set
boldly on a raised platform in the center of the
stage. A Jessner production designed by Cesar
Klein.

actors and furniture and of actors and actors. Nobody notes his shortcomings in this regard. Put him upon an almost naked stage, and he must not only make his actors far more expressive in voice and feature, but he must also do fine things with their bodies and their meager surroundings. This is far easier for a pictorial artist than for the director, who is usually an actor without a well-trained eye. The director must therefore employ an artist even in the sceneryless theater, and employ him to do what is really a work of direction. The two must try to fuse their individualities and abilities, and bring out a composite director-artist, a double man possessing the talents that appear together in Pitoëff.

The immediate question is obviously this: If the director cannot acquire the talents of the artist, why cannot the artist acquire the talents of the director? If the knack of visual design, and the keen appreciation of physical relationships cannot be cultivated in a man who does not possess them by birth, is it likewise impossible for the man who possesses them to acquire the faculty of understanding and of drawing forth emotion in the actor?

The problem narrows down to the temperament of the artist *versus* the temperament of the director. There is a difference; it is no use denying it. The director is ordinarily a man sensitive enough to understand human emotion deeply and to be able to recognize it, summon it, and guide it in actors. But he must also be callous enough to meet the contacts of direction —often very difficult contacts—and to organize not only the performance of the players, but also a great deal of bothersome detail involving men and women who must be managed and cajoled, commanded, and worn down, and generally treated as no artist cares to treat others, or to treat himself in the process of treating others. The director must be an executive, and this implies a cold ability to dominate other human beings, which the artist does not ordinarily have. The artist is essentially a lonely worker. He is not gregarious in his labor.

So far as the future goes, the hope for the artist is that he will be able to reverse the Butlerian process which held in the relations of director and designer. He must be able to "grow a director." This may not be so very difficult. It may very well happen that an artist will employ a stage manager, as an astute director now employs an artist, to do a part of his work for him. He will explain to the stage manager the general scheme of production that he wants, much as a director explains to an artist the sort of settings he desires. The stage manager will rehearse the movements of the actors towards this end. When the artist sees opportunities for further development of action and business, he will explain this to the stage manager, and perhaps to the players involved, and the stage manager will again see that the ideas of his superior are carried out. Something of the kind occurs even now where a director employs a sub-

The first scene from *Othello* as staged by Leopold
Jessner in Berlin. On long curved steps which
remain throughout, and against the neutral background of the cyclorama, the artist, Emil Pirchan,
puts the barest indications of place. Here, Braban-
tio's house gleams like a moonstone against a background of neutral-tinted distance.

director to "break in" the company. Both Reinhardt and Arthur Hopkins, though thoroughly capable of "wading into" a group of players, and enforcing action by minute direction and imitation, generally use the quiet method of consulting with players, and suggesting changes to them, not during the actual rehearsal, but afterwards in the protection of a wing or the privacy of a dressing room.

The presence of the artist as director in some future theater without scenery, implies a decided influence on the type of acting.

Such a stage itself, thrust boldly at the spectators, if not actually placed in the midst of them, tends to dictate a frank, direct contact between players and audience. In such a house an actor will be all but forced to desert the purely representational style of to-day, and to present himself and his emotions in an open, assertive, masculine manner as objects of art and of emotion.

The tendency of the artist towards this kind of theater implies, I think, a tendency towards presentational acting. Certainly I have talked with few who were not receptive to it.

Put together a stage that tends towards presentational acting and an artist whose instincts run to the same ends, and the outcome is not difficult to foresee.

The problem at present is, what artist? And where? And how soon?

CHAPTER XI

A NEW ADVENTURE IN DIRECTION

THE outstanding director in the German theater to-day is also the most radical director. And the most radical director is at the head of the Prussian State Theater, the Schauspielhaus, in Berlin. His name is Leopold Jessner, and he is the only man who has threatened to fill the place made vacant by Reinhardt's retirement. Some say that he has already filled it, and—with disarming logic—that Reinhardt was only a mountebank anyhow. Some think Jessner a clever eccentric. Certainly he is the most discussed personality in the German theater, and his methods are the most debated.

One word crops up whenever his name is mentioned—*Jessnertreppen*. The German language has boiled down into a single word an idea that we would have to phrase as "those crazy steps of Leopold Jessner." It makes a handy stone for the anti-Jessnerites to throw at the director's friends. Jessner's friends are beginning to have the good sense to pick up the stone and throw it back. For the word *Jessnertreppen* hits off a virtue—perhaps the main virtue of the man.

Jessner fills his stage with steps. He seems unable to get

130

Othello: act III, scene 3. A towering column, with its lower end sharpened like the point of a lead pencil, is seemingly driven into one end of the central platform. Othello and Iago stand at the base.

IAGO: Have you not sometimes seen a handkerchief
Spotted with strawberries in your wife's
hands?

along without them. He must have platforms, levels, walls, terraces. They are to him what screens, towering shapes, great curtains are to Gordon Craig. In every production Jessner, through his artist, Emil Pirchan, provides some permanent foundation besides the stage-floor for the actor to play upon, some arrangement of different levels. In his *Richard III* it is a wall all across the stage, with a platform along the top at the base of another wall, and for certain scenes a flight of steps like a pyramid placed against the lower wall. In *Othello* Jessner uses two platforms, one on top of the other, each reached by two or three steps, the lower a long ellipse almost as large as the stage, the upper one smaller and proportionately broader; upon the upper platform Jessner places certain indications of setting. For Grabbe's *Napoleon* he uses four or five steps rising sharply to a platform perhaps four feet high. Sometimes this platform is supplemented by a high one pulled apart in the middle to make opposing hills, redoubts, vantage points in the battle scenes.

The *Jessnertreppen* are the key to the physical things in this director's productions. They give the stage one general shape for each play. They establish a formal quality. They tend to banish representation in scenery, since only indications of setting harmonize with their frank artificiality. And— their main purpose—they provide the director with most interesting opportunities for manœuvering his actors.

131

One of the simplest and most obvious of these is a new way of making entrances. Such steps as are used in *Othello* and *Napoleon* go down at the back as far as they rise in the front, and below that the director opens a trap or two in the floor. Thus he is able to have an actor walk straight up out of the back of the stage, and appear in a dominating position in the middle of the action. Jessner uses this novel means of entrance again and again in *Othello*, and it is always fresh and effective. For the return to Cyprus the Moor marches triumphantly up these steps, to the welcome of his wife.

Far more important, however, is what Jessner does with the front of the steps. They may be there to help a formal stage with very little scenery to seem steadily interesting even to audiences that expect the conventional gauds of the theater. But their true office is to make possible a sort of three-dimensional direction for which Jessner has become renowned. Ordinarily the actor moves in only two directions upon the stage—right and left, and towards the footlights and away from them. As a matter of fact, the latter movement is so unsatisfactory from the point of view of any spectators except those in the balconies, that the actor really has only one plane in which he can move visibly and expressively. Jessner does more than add a third dimension when he sends his actors up and down the steps. He also gives a great deal more significance to the movement towards and away from the audience.

Othello: act 4, scene 2. Cyprus. The castle.
On the central platform are set two curved screens
of dull salmon pink. Behind, the quivering darkness of the unlighted cyclorama. Emilia, dressed
in deep crimson, stands in the foreground.

Beside the sense of movement—always an intriguing thing in the theater—Jessner provides in his steps a mechanism for solving many dramatic problems. His actors do not spend their time getting out of the way of the actors behind them. They are not shuttling back and forth in an effort to let the audience see all the players at the same time. One actor cannot "cover" another if he stands on steps. Even a very large crowd can appear on such a stage without the individual speakers being lost. As Lee Simonson showed in his use of different levels for the Theater Guild's production of *He Who Gets Slapped*, with the proper sort of elevations on the stage a large number of actors can play a very complicated scene without confusing their relationships or assuming awkward positions.

But a great deal more important than this negative virtue is the positive contribution of steps in permitting many more and much finer compositions than the flat floor permits. Jessner composes freely in three dimensions. He composes both for esthetic and for dramatic effect.

There are times when you can see him arranging his actors with nothing but the esthetic aim in mind. Take the first scene in which Napoleon himself appears in Grabbe's drama. It is not a particularly good setting in some ways; it is a rather obvious and ugly silhouette of a bastion and a slanting parapet leading up to it. The scene shows Napoleon receiving reports

133

from an officer and giving orders. Jessner deliberately places Napoleon on top of the bastion against the sky and stands the officer stiffly on the parapet below; the relation of the two men as characters in the play is thus established visually as well as through the text. The relation of the two men as a composition—not as characters—has to be disturbed by the entrance of a second officer. It is obviously impossible for Napoleon and the first officer both to retain their positions if the second officer is to fit into a composition. Accordingly the first moves just enough to establish a new esthetic relation embracing all three.

Jessner is free with his dramatic compositions and occasionally altogether too obvious. He keeps his dominant people at the top of the *Jessnertreppen*, or brings them down as they lose command. He handles the accession of Richard III as Shakespeare did, and as very few directors have since done. When the burghers come to ask Richard to be king, they find him "aloft, between two bishops," in compliance with Buckingham's advice: "Go, go up to the leads." Jessner has Richard walk upon the platform above the wall; it is his first appearance on high and he maintains his place until the battle at the end. At the close of *Napoleon*, the emperor, who has appeared hitherto only at the top of the steps, is seen seated, broken and disconsolate, on the lowest step of all, with a sinking sun behind him, and the soldiers above.

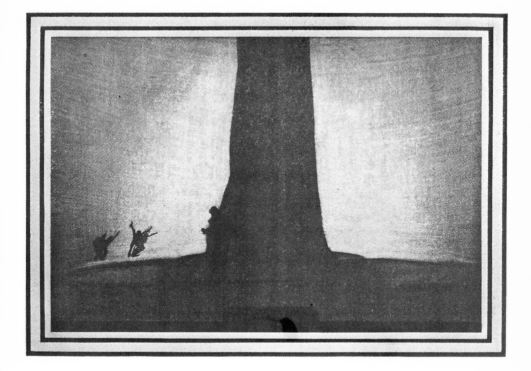

Othello: act 4, scene 2. Iago lurks in the shadow of a great black shape distorted like the trunk of some fantastic tree. Cassio pursues Roderigo along a narrow path which skirts the base of the cyclorama; you see their running figures, far away and small.

It would seem safe to infer from all this that Jessner is not a realistic producer. He might, of course, have achieved many of these effects within a natural setting, but only at the cost of a great deal of laborious planning and manœuvering. As a matter of fact, Jessner doesn't use one ounce of energy trying to be either natural or plausible. His method is openly expressionistic.

Jessner distorts the natural in a hundred ways to achieve something expressive of the drama. The first scene in *Napoleon*, as he gives it, is supposed according to the text to pass in the arcades of the Palais Royal, lined with booths. Various episodes, dialogues, and harangues take place between different speakers and different knots of the crowd. The usual method of handling such a scene is to turn on and off the speech of the different groups of actors at will, making certain speakers and parts of the crowd obligingly inaudible to the audience. There is little enough of nature in such a business, but Jessner banishes even that. He keeps the stage empty except for small crowds that rush out, along with the speakers or show-barkers, for particular episodes.

Jessner handles crowds even more arbitrarily at times. Later in *Napoleon*, during a riot preceding the news of Napoleon's return from exile, a revolutionist kills a tailor. As his body sinks to the steps, the crowd of red-clothed men and women falls upon him, almost as if to devour the corpse, and covers the steps as with a great blood-red stain. In *Richard III*, when Gloucester appears as king in a red cloak upon the top of the red steps, which are placed for this purpose against the wall, his eight retainers, also in red, sink down in a heap below him like a pile of bloody skulls. In *Othello*, when the Moor returns in triumph to Cyprus a cheering crowd comes with him up the steps from the back. When he has reached the top and can go no higher, the crowd sinks prostrate. For a moment he seems to grow in stature, and his triumph to tower upward.

These are all compositions in three dimensions, as well as violations of ordinary human conduct. Jessner can also create symbolic action out of unnatural action without any particular aid from the steps. The scene of Napoleon's entrance into the throne room of Louis XVIII is an interesting example. The steps give prominence to the throne, and enable the audience to see better; but Jessner's symbolism has nothing to do with the steps. The scene is made up of some curtains masking each side, two wings cut in rococo curves and ornamented with lilies in rococo patterns. A flat backdrop of the same design and colors—not a very good design or very French colors —completes the room. In this room in an earlier scene Louis has held audience, a fat, yellow-and-white egg of a man, like some Humpty-Dumpty caught in a flood of the fierce white light that is supposed to beat about a throne, and all too seldom

The prison scene from *Richard III*. A triangular
patch of light discloses a low arched opening in
the nearer wall of the permanent setting where
Clarence sits in chains.

CLARENCE: Wedges of gold, great anchors, heaps
of pearl,
Inestimable stones, unvalued jewels. . . .

does anything of the kind. But now Louis is gone, and the lilies of the wall are shadowed by curtains of Napoleonic blue, which have, for some unaccountable reason, got themselves hung in the room. Napoleon enters through the gap in the curtains, reaches up, seizes the edge of one of them, and pulls it down over the glory that was Bourbon. Then he turns and faces the audience while two files of soldiers march stiffly past him to the opposite side from which each entered. The gesture to the curtains, and the *staccato* march of the soldiers back of Napoleon, set out the drama of his returning power.

Naturally Shakespeare, even more than Grabbe, gives Jessner exceptional opportunities to symbolize and formalize in direction. He is quick to seize them—particularly in the soliloquies. He begins *Richard III* with Gloucester speaking to the audience as Prologue; he ends it with Richmond as Epilogue. Jessner always flings asides directly at the spectators. When he comes upon soliloquies—as in Brakenbury's musings after Clarence has fallen asleep in his cell—he cuts them off sharply from the previous action by altering the lighting, and bringing the actor down-stage to speak full at the audience. He places the murderers squatting on the prompter's box for much of their chatter. He has the scrivener read Hastings' condemnation to the audience from the same vantage point, and upon this relic, in poses fashioned a little after Rodin's *Burghers of Calais*, he places the three citizens who discourse of the old king's death and the sorry state of the realm.

Jessner is quite as arbitrary in his handling of light as in his handling of people. He does not use light merely to illumine the stage, as directors did thirty years ago. He does not use light and shadow merely to define action by making faces and figures more dynamic, as Appia set modern producers doing. He uses light and shadow as a parallel expression to the play. Light and shadow act the drama almost as much as do the players. The light is not in the least "natural." It suits the mood of the scene. It waxes and wanes with the progress or the action. When the little princes enter in *Richard III* the light shines out more brightly. When Othello dies, it grows dim, then a sharp shaft of light shoots out from the prompter's box, and throws the shadow of Iago over the tragedy he has caused, and the shadow of the great canopied bed spreads out over the cyclorama, which has stood as a sort of limit of space about the play. Jessner is particularly fond of shadows. When one rival meets another and vanquishes him, Jessner will have him literally "throw him into the shade." Spotlights, flashing on, create meaningful shadows. An amusing example occurs in the soliloquy of Richard ending:

> Shine out, fair sun, till I have bought a glass,
> That I may see my shadow as I pass.

138

Richard III: Gloucester and his shadow.   A high
green-gray wall extends straight across the stage;
in front, a lower wall.   As Gloucester speaks,

> Shine out, fair sun, till I have bought a glass,
> That I may see my shadow as I pass,

a spotlight concealed in the prompter's box is suddenly turned on and his shadow looms up, huge
and sinister.

As Richard says this, the lights on the stage go down, and a spotlight from the prompter's box throws his humped shadow on the wall.

Jessner has his players under unusual control, and he permits very little of the accidental expression of feeling which Gordon Craig inveighs against in the actor. He even forbids the little shiftings and motions of the hands which are natural to anybody, actor or layman, while listening to a long speech from another. Jessner's actors, if they are not speaking, and if their emotions are not being very markedly played upon, are held motionless. They do not move a limb. I have heard that, in a ball room scene, Jessner kept dozens of players absolutely immobile in the poses of the dance while the two principals talked.

Jessner's company, as it appears in *Richard III*, *Napoleon*, and *Othello*, displays no extraordinary talent. The director has instilled a vitality as sharp as the silence and immobility which he frequently demands; and they play with that drive and that sharpness of accent which are inherently German. But there is no genius here, no Moissi.

Fritz Kortner, who plays Richard and Othello, is the outstanding figure, but he seems a player of limited vision and not very great technical range. He plays both parts on the same two notes: a soft, precise, and almost whispering voice, and another that rasps and all but squalls. Both are a little

139

monotonous in tempo and accent. He uses the voice of the dove a great deal in *Othello*, both to establish the Moor's kind and noble nature, and also as a base upon which to rear the contrast of his anger. The dove is a serpent in *Richard*.

Physically, Kortner's Richard is odd and striking. The actor is not very tall, and he is decidedly thick in figure. His attitudes, the apelike swing of his arms, his pudgy face, twisted by an evil grin, give him an odd appearance that constantly suggests other images than Richard himself. A humped toad, a fat, cross monkey, a grinning Japanese mask, the mask of a Greek comedian—finally the truth strikes home: it is the *Balzac* of Rodin.

There is a moment in *Richard* when this curious figure is forgotten. It is the dream of the king the night before the battle of Bosworth Field. (Why is it, by the way, that no producer seems to have the genius and naïveté to produce this scene as Shakespeare wrote it, to place the tents of Richard and of Richmond on either side of the stage, and to let the ghosts bless Richmond and curse Richard alternately as they do in the text?) Jessner shears away the blessings, and lets the ghosts curse in the wings. Upon the slant of the blood-red steps lies Richard sleeping. As the voices call, he writhes and twists upon his uneasy couch. The voices rise and race, his agitation grows more and more horrible, until at the end his humped body is beating a fearsome tattoo to the rhythm of

140

Richard III: Gloucester becomes King. Robed in scarlet, he stands at the head of a flight of blood-red steps. Below him, a double row of kneeling, scarlet-clad courtiers. Behind, a high gray wall. Above, a blood-red sky.

the cursing ghostly voices. Immediately after this really effective and fine scene, comes the extraordinary, much talked of and quite ludicrous end of Richard. He has his scene with the generals, then goes off to battle—or is it merely to tear off his coat of mail and his shirt? At any rate he is on the stage a few moments later, staggering along the top of the wall, naked to the waist. He cries: "A horse! a horse! my kingdom for a horse!" Then he mounts his sword and, as if on a hobby horse, hops down the steps until exhaustion overcomes him and he falls.

Perhaps this indicates the fault that at present keeps Jessner from being a great director. His judgment and his taste—which mean the soul with which he interprets and animates his work—are very, very faulty. There is no austerity and almost no true beauty in his *Othello*, only strength. There is no dignity in his *Richard III*, only horror. He has made Richard terrible, but only with the terror of wormy graveyards. There is nothing of 15th century England in it, none of the beauty and flash of the time to make the hideousness of Gloucester the darker. The play is drowned in black—dirty, mean black. Far worse, it is stripped of the qualities that are Shakespeare. Worst of all, there is no shred of poetry in the whole length of the production, unless it is the final moment.

If you can forget the question of taste—if you do not care what interpretation a man puts on a great work of art—you

141

must admit Jessner to a very high place as a director. He has originality, ingenuity, bravery, an uncommon technical ability. He is industrious, and indefatigably careful. His sins are not the sins of Reinhardt. No detail escapes him; so small a thing as off-stage noise he handles with the greatest skill. But Jessner is no poet.

With the question of taste goes also another fault, not so grave, yet important and perhaps significant. Jessner appears to worship the obvious, to believe that the theater is a place of A. B. C. impressions and reactions. He is daring enough in his technique but not in his ideas. He flings out symbols right and left, but they are the symbols of the primer. He directs in words of one syllable. *Richard III* is an explanation in black and white, which occasionally ventures to lisp in white and red. Richard begins the play in black against a black curtain, speaking the soliloquy of "Now is the winter of our discontent." Richmond ends it in white against a white curtain with his speech to Stanley and his soldiers converted into a soliloquy to the audience. The troops of Richard are red-clothed figures crossing the red steps. The troops of Richmond cross it in white. This is symbolism in baby-talk, presentational production in kindergarten terms. It is not impossible that an audience is up to more than that.

It may be, of course, that Jessner is feeling his way and that to-morrow he will venture upon subtlety—if it is in him. At

142

Richard III: on the blood-red steps of Richard's coronation stands Richmond, a white-robed general at the head of an army all in white.

any rate, here is a presentational director, a man who forswears resemblance and the picture frame, and who sets actors and their movements, the setting and its lights, talking directly to the audience. This is an advance in the methods of production which makes the new movement of twenty years ago look like an afternoon stroll, a revolt which makes that much-hailed revolution seem a pleasant little excursion. It is an advance and a revolt, however, still looking for a leader.

143

CHAPTER XII

MASSE-MENSCH—MOB-MAN

PROPHECY is a risky business in the theater, especially when prophecy concerns itself with personalities rather than tendencies. I find it very difficult to bring myself to say that the man who will become the leader of the new forces in the Continental theater is Jürgen Fehling, director of *Masse-Mensch*. And yet—on the basis of a single production —the temptation to believe something of the kind is strong indeed.

Fehling's work is closely associated with two striking phenomena. One is the Volksbühne, the workingman's theatrical organization of Berlin, which maintains the handsomest and best devised theater in the German capital; and the other is the play which has been given there with such uncommon success, *Masse-Mensch*, a strange and powerful tragedy of the "social revolution of the twentieth century" written by a communist leader, Ernst Toller.

The Berlin Volksbühne is interesting enough in itself. As the only organization that has been able to produce successfully this expressionist tragedy of communism, its power and

144

The first moment of Jessner's *Richard III*. Gloucester, a grotesque, twisted figure in black, stands silhouetted against a black curtain. In contrast to this Richmond speaks the final lines of the play dressed in white against a white curtain.

GLOUCESTER: Now is the winter of our discontent
Made glorious summer. . . .

Between these two extremes of black on black and white on white the play takes its course.

position seem highly significant. This society of proletarian
playgoers was founded more than thirty years ago as a sprouting
bed for naturalistic drama and the social thesis-play. To-day
it still cultivates the best in Realism and in the social drama,
but it looks condescendingly on the thesis-play, and it gives the
most completely artistic and successful example to be seen in
Germany of an expressionist play and an expressionist production.

The Volksbühne has always had a double policy—that
of buying out performances of good plays and retailing the
seats to its members for much less than the box office prices, and
that of producing plays itself. It began with a few Sunday performances of both kinds, and steadily grew in membership to
the point where it buys all the Sunday matinees at a number
of theaters, has two playhouses of its own, the Volksbühne and
the Neues Volkstheater, and is organizing an opera house, the
Volksoper. One hundred and eighty thousand men and women
of the lower and lower-middle classes subscribed in 1922 for
eight productions, either at the society's theaters or at the playhouses with which it deals.

The Volksbühne itself is rather an extraordinary theater.
Its striking front, with the words *Die Kunst dem Volke* upon
its pediment, rises across a street that cuts through the working-
men's quarter of Berlin, and, after a slight bend, crosses the
Spree and becomes Unter den Linden. From above its little

triangle of park, the Volksbühne stares ironically and, doubtless, a little proudly down the long street that passes the hideous art galleries of the Prussian government, the palaces once occupied by the Hohenzollerns, the State Opera, where royalty turned its back upon Richard Strauss, and runs on to the Brandenburger Tor of Imperial memories. The theater has the grimly noble air of the best of German architecture. In its auditorium Oskar Kaufmann has turned from the austerity of gray stone to the richness of red mahogany. The working class audiences of the Volksbühne find themselves seated, therefore, in the handsomest and doubtless the most costly auditorium of Berlin when they come to see the play which might almost be the story of their own defeat in the communist risings of 1919.

Masse-Mensch itself is a play, half dream and half reality, in which is pictured the conflict of *Masse*, the masses, against *Mensch*, the individual, of violent revolution against passive strike. Its drama pleads piteously for the sacredness of human life and the equal guilt of the State or the revolution that takes it. Because it was written by Ernst Toller, who, as he wrote it, lay in a Munich jail serving a twenty-year sentence for his part as Minister of Justice in the red rebellion which followed the assassination of Kurt Eisner by the reactionaries, *Masse-Mensch* is pretty generally taboo in German theaters. In the first six months after its *première* at the Volksbühne (29th September, 1921) it was played about seventy times, a

146

Richard III: the final moment. White virtue triumphs.

RICHMOND: Now civil wounds are stopp'd, Peace lives again:
That she may long live here, God say Amen!

very great number of performances in repertory. But upon its production in Nuremberg riots interrupted the first performance, and it was never repeated.

To the significance of the play itself and the proletarian organization which flings it in the face of a Germany where monarchists and republicans, socialists and communists, State and cabals, murder with almost equal recklessness, must be added a truly remarkable type and quality of production. It bears a certain relation to the work of Jessner at the State Schauspielhaus, where, by the way, Fehling is now to be employed. It is absolutely free of Realism and representation— as all expressionist production must be. It reduces setting to less than symbol, to what is hardly more than a convenient platform for the actor. It uses light arbitrarily.

Masse-Mensch is a piece in seven scenes. The first, third, fifth and seventh are actual; the others are dream-pictures. In the first scene Toller's stage directions call for "The rear room of a workingman's meeting hall. On the white-washed walls, portraits of leaders of the people and photographs of union delegates. In the center a heavy table, at which a woman and two workmen are seated." The stage directions for the second scene, or first dream-picture, read: "Indicated: The hall of a stock exchange. At the desk, a clerk; about him, bankers and brokers."

The playwright felt keenly the possibilities of the modern,

147

subjective methods of productions, or he would not have used the word, "indicated." He did not feel them clearly enough, however, to risk more than their application to the dream-pictures. But, taking "Indicated" as a key-word, Fehling has boldly ventured to apply abstract and expressionist methods to the whole of this thoroughly expressionist play. In the first scene, for instance, as you see it at the Volksbühne, there is no hall, there is no desk, there are no portraits. There is nothing but a deep box of high black curtains, and in the center a very low, broad platform. Upon this platform, spotted out with three shafts of light, are the two men and the woman in the taut attitudes of wrestlers as they clasp hands, the woman in the middle. For the dream scene, the stage is again in black curtains, but those at the rear are occasionally opened to show a clerk on an impossibly high stool, writing on an impossibly high desk, almost in silhouette against the yellow-lighted dome. A few steps lead down into the darkness of the front stage. Fehling and his stage designer, Hans Strohbach, pursue the same general method in the succeeding scenes. The "real" episodes are set in black curtains and with steps of one sort or another; they are lit by obvious beams of light, and they are given no more color than shows in the woman's severe blue dress and one glimpse of the yellow dome. The dream-pictures are more elaborately staged, though they seem quite bare by the standard of our productions. The curious part is that the

Masse-Mensch: dream-picture. A courtyard. Towering dark walls lean inward; a green night sky; guards with lanterns seated on the floor at either side. A man stands in the center playing a concertina.

scenes of reality are more expressionistic, considering their purpose, than the dream-pictures. Reality is made of nothing but abstract plastic shapes, harsh, and harshly lit. Dreamland is sometimes painted and shaped in the slightly decorative spirit of Expressionism, and it is lit with beauty and atmosphere.

The effective arrangement of Strohbach's scenes, and the powerful use which Fehling makes of them stamp the physical side of this production with distinction. Spiritually it is even more distinguished because of the rightness of vision with which Fehling interprets the play, and the brilliance with which he handles, not only the individual acting, but a chorus of united voices, which speaks through many scenes with an extraordinary clarity and emotion.

From the beginning of the first scene the actors strike the note of intensity and conviction, both as players and as characters, which they are to carry through the whole performance. Mary Dietrich, once of Reinhardt's company, plays superbly the woman protagonist of the strike and of humanity. From the moment when her husband comes to her in the name of love to ask her to give up the leadership of the strike, which will begin next day, Dietrich drives with such furious precision at the meaning of this woman that she stands out immediately as a sort of Christ-figure. In the beginning she must give up all; she must leave home and love, to follow her call. In the end she must go to the scaffold rejecting all means of escape. It is one of the distinctions of this play, as well as of Dietrich's playing, that this reference to Christ is so beautiful and so sure, yet so reticent.

The second scene, the dream-picture of a stock exchange, is a foreboding and dread satire. The bankers and brokers bid up human souls in the war that is under way, and make plans for an international corporation, which, posing as a founder of homes for convalescent soldiers, will open brothels for the troops. The woman appears in her dream, and makes a vain appeal to the humanity of these men. The bankers hear only the announcement of a mine accident and plan a benefit dance, beginning with a fox-trot by the brokers around the stage.

The third scene is the labor meeting at which a decision is to be taken on action to stop the making of munitions and end the war. Here again, Fehling throws the author's realistic stage directions overboard (much, be it said, to the author's pleasure). Instead of a hall, there is again blackness, emptiness. Out of the emptiness speaks a marvelous choral voice, the voice of the masses, measured, vibrant, intense:

> Wir ewig eingekeilt
> In Schluchten steiler Häuser.
> Wir preisgegeben
> Der Mechanik höhnischer Systeme.
> Wir antlitzlos in Nacht der Tränen.
> Wir ewig losgelöst von Müttern,

Masse-Mensch: the revolutionists' meeting. On
a broad flight of steps rising steeply from the footlights, men and women are grouped in an irregular lozenge, arbitrarily lit by sharp beams of light
from the top and sides of the proscenium arch.
A Fehling production designed by Strohbach.

MASSE-MENSCH—MOB-MAN

Aus Tiefen der Fabriken rufen wir:
Wann werden Liebe wir leben?
Wann werden Werk wir wirken?
Wann wird Erlösung uns?

Nothing like this voice, coming out of a darkness in which faces vaguely begin to hover, has been imagined, much less attempted, in our theater. The lights rise—or it would be more accurate to say, shoot down—upon the men and women workers standing in an irregular lozenge shape upon steep steps, which spread to the curtains at each side. Out of this crowd, in chorus and singly, come pleas for action, and visions of suffering which sweep the audience with emotion. The woman cries for a strike against war and against capital. Behind her rises The Nameless One, the bastard of War, to cry for armed revolt. His passion sweeps the masses, and the woman submits.

The fourth scene, another dream-picture, envisages her fears for the course of the revolution, her intuition that it will only breed a new violence, the violence of the proletariat. Below great, crooked, towering walls, guards hang over green lanterns. They sing ribald songs of their miseries. The Nameless One enters, and, standing in the middle, plays wildly on a concertina, while the guards and the condemned dance the dance of death about him. The sky lights up on a sudden in crimson, then pulses in and out; colors flood down over the moving figures in waves that throb with the music. Among the condemned is

151

the husband of the woman.   She tries to save him, as she would save all men from violence.   Her pleas are useless.   She stands with him before the firing squad as the curtain falls.

The fifth scene, the tremendous scene of the play and the production, is the rally at the workers' headquarters in the face of defeat.   The stage is again boxed in black.   There are steps like the corner of a pyramid rising up to the right of the audience.   Upon these steps gather the working people.   You see a host, affrighted and cowering, in the twenty-four men and women who stagger upon the steps singing *The Marseillaise*. As they sway, locked together hand in hand, like men on a sinking ship, and the old song mounts up against the distant rattle of machine guns, the scene brings the cold sweat of desperate excitement to the audience that fills the Volksbühne, and to comfortable, purse-proud Americans as much as to men who have fought in the streets of Berlin.   Suddenly there is a louder rattle of arms.   The noise sweeps through the air.   It drives into the souls of the huddling men and women.   They collapse, go down, fall in a tangled heap.   The curtains at the left loop up suddenly.   There in the gap against the yellow sky stand the soldiers.   They arrest the woman, the woman whom the rebels were about to condemn for her opposition to their slaughter.

The sixth scene is a dream-picture of the woman in prison. There is a void, a misty, swimming emptiness.   Upon a plat-

Masse-Mensch: the rallying. A pyramid of steps slanting to the right of the stage. At its apex, a group of tense revolutionists sing *The Marseillaise,* the woman-heroine opposite them in the center. Suddenly machine-guns attack the meeting.

form is the woman's cell, a scarlet cage in which she can only kneel. About her stand guards, bankers, the ghosts of dead enemies. They accuse her. She answers. At last, out of the void rise the shapes of the masses, the imprisoned masses who have been betrayed by violence and by the woman who deserted them and cast her lot with violence. They move in a great circle of towering shadows that seem to hang in the emptiness of the sky, as they pass across the dome at the back of the stage. The guilt of the masses, the guilt of the individual, the guilt of the woman—they have filled the air with recrimination. The figures of the imprisoned masses stop suddenly in their round. They raise their arms. They cry: "We accuse!"

There is only the final scene left. It is in her cell. Again the black curtains; some narrow steps. The husband comes to bring her freedom. The Nameless One also, with a plan of escape through murdering the guards. She rejects both. She rejects the priest, accusing men of primeval sin. She goes to her death. And as she goes, two women prisoners sneak out into the light—to divide the clothes of this new Christ.

Schuldig! Guilty! Guilty! The word echoes through the play, echoes in the auditorium of the Volksbühne. All are guilty. All are sick with guilt. And none more than these sufferers in the slums of Berlin who must go to the theater to see in black curtains the picture of their guilt. The world goes

153

through capitalism, debasing itself, driving terror, greed, cruelty into the place of love and understanding. It comes out in revolution, a corruption of the thing it cures. The Germans have been through capitalism with a vengeance, through materialism, through war, and through a revolution that blasted half the people and did not satisfy the rest. Here is the misery of capitalism, the misery of abortive revolution, the misery of defeat and black hunger. Berlin is in purgatory. And Berlin goes to *Masse-Mensch*. Before this play sit hundreds of quite ordinary men, who have only to hear some word shouted at them with the passion of this play, and they will leave the slow and loved routine of homes, and lie again behind sandbags on Unter den Linden. All this is a strange, terrible, and sweet thing to feel as you sit looking at the purgatory of those black curtains.

Toller and Fehling have made possible the realization of this intense situation between play and audience; Toller by writing straight at the heart of his public. His dialogue makes no pretense to the accidental rhythms of life. It speaks out plainly and simply and beautifully the passion of each character, the passions of the world. Fehling has driven Toller's speeches just as directly at the public. He has made no pretense at actuality. He has put his actors forward as actors on an abstract stage; and you think of them only as living, intimate presences.

Comparison between Fehling and Jessner is inevitable.

Masse-Mensch: the machine-guns. The black
curtains at the back are thrown open. Soldiers
and officers are seen enveloped in a thin haze of
smoke. The group shrinks back and falls together.

They are both working upon the newest problem of production, the problem of escaping from Realism to reality and to the theater. They both throw overboard every shred of actuality that stands in the way of inner emotional truth. Technically, Fehling is as insistent as Jessner on the abstract, the formal production as the means of giving the actor and his emotion vividly and completely to the audience. Fehling realizes as keenly as Jessner does how different playing-levels can help him in deploying and emphasizing his actors. He does not, like Jessner, use the same levels throughout a play. He creates new plastics as he needs them. His production is formal in principle, but he does not rely upon a stage of certain permanent forms. His lighting is abstract, like Jessner's, paying no attention at all to actuality; but it is not so free or so wilful in changes. The lights make a definite pattern in each scene and stick to it throughout. The only sharp exception is the scene of the dance of the condemned. Fehling does not try to make his lighting a running gloss to the words of the play.

Fehling may be much over-praised by the emotion of *Masse-Mensch*; perhaps there is a something in the passion of the play which lights up these players and these playgoers of the Volksbühne, and brings forth a unique and unwilled emotion. But there seem to be certain qualities in this production which stamp the director as a man of imagination and power. Certainly Fehling has a large and healthful simpleness. He isn't finicking over rudimentary explanations with lights and shadows and primary colors. He isn't missing the quality of the play in an endeavor to create a thing of a single startling or novel tone. He is certainly winning from his actors a spiritual coöperation finer than any that we saw in Germany. He is unmistakably one of the leaders along new paths—a sure and challenging force.

Masse-Mensch: A woman dressed in blue in a dream-prison of twisted scarlet bars, surrounded by motionless dark figures. Behind, gigantic spectral shadow-shapes march across a faintly luminous void.

CHAPTER XIII

"THE THEATER OF THE FIVE THOUSAND"

OVER some fifteen years a growing number of minds have been more or less actively seeking a way towards a new type of theater. They have been abusing the picture-frame stage, stamping on the footlights, pulling out the front of the apron, pushing the actors into the loges, down the orchestra pit, onto the prompter's box, out upon runways or up the aisles. They have even gone clear out of the playhouse and into circuses, open air theaters, and public parks. All to set up a new and mutual relationship between the actor and the audience.

You might almost say to set up any mutual relationship at all; for the players of the peephole theater of Realism, the picture-frame theater, the fourth wall theater, can hardly be said to have anything resembling a relationship to the spectator. The thing peeped at can't be aware of the peeper. A picture does not know that it has an audience. Walls may have ears, but the fourth wall has no eyes. It is the essence of Realism and of realistic acting that they have their justification in the thing they resemble, not in the people who may or may

157

not be able to recognize the resemblance. A perfect realistic performance is a thing so close to life that it cannot permit itself to be aware of even its own existence. Its perfection is so much more related to the thing it imitates than to the audience which looks at it, that it would be no less perfect if there were no one at all to look. The fourth wall *is* a fourth wall. It might just as well be as real as the other three. Alexander Bakshy wrote of Stanislavsky's company: "It would have made scarcely an atom of difference to the adequacy and completeness of the Art Theater's performance if the audience had been entirely removed."

Such performances can be very interesting in their way, extraordinarily interesting, in fact, when such players as Stanislavsky's bring spiritual distinction to their Realism. But there is another sort of thing that can be interesting, too. Some think it can be more interesting; at any rate they want to find out what it was that kept the theater contented for the twenty-five centuries before it knew Realism. They want to draw out the actor and the spectator; the actor out of the picture frame and the spectator—if the actor is good enough—out of his seat. They want to make the actor an actor once more. And they think that a new sort of theater—or a very old sort—might have something to do with it.

Directors have thought about it, and playwrights, dancing teachers, architects, scenic artists, actors, and critics. Max

Reinhardt put a runway over the audience in *Sumurûn* more than a dozen years ago and staged Sophocles in a circus. Percy MacKaye developed the community masque as a new form of outdoor theatrical performance through *The Masque of St. Louis* and *Caliban*, and brought it indoors with *The Evergreen Tree* and *The Will of Song*. Jaques-Dalcroze, deviser of the eurythmic system of dance-education, created in Hellerau-bei-Dresden, before the war, a hall holding the stage and the spectators within translucent walls lit by ten thousand lights, and there, with the aid of Adolphe Appia, he gave Paul Claudel's drama *L'Annonce faite à Marie*. Frank Lloyd Wright, designing a theater for Aline Barnsdall of Los Angeles, created a model showing an adjustable proscenium, which was hardly a proscenium, a domed stage which curved into the lines of the auditorium, and a permanent architectural setting consisting of a wall twelve feet high running across the stage. Herman Rosse, the scenic artist, took to sketching theaters with all manner of odd forestages and portals. Norman-Bel Geddes threw off in 1914 a plan for a theater with stage and audience housed under a single dome, and in 1921 designed a magnificent project for the production of Dante's *The Divine Comedy* in Madison Square Garden in a permanent setting of ringed steps, towering plinths, and light. Gémier, the French actor, introduced the Reinhardt circus-theater to Paris. Jacques Copeau left his reviewing of plays to create in the Vieux-Colombier a theater without a proscenium, and with a forestage and a permanent setting, in order to give his troupe of actors a fresh and truly theatrical relation to their audience.

The first attempts to escape from the realistic theater were Gargantuan. It seems as if there were something so essentially small about our theater that a huge thing was the natural alternative. Max Reinhardt and Percy MacKaye, the two men who began the break with the realistic theater, and who carried their conceptions furthest, plunged immediately to the huge, the magnificent. They could have found inspiration in Gordon Craig, as practically every innovator in our playhouse has done. For Gordon Craig, too, saw a gigantic vision of the break between this peepshow of ours and the next theater:

"I see a great building to seat many thousands of people. At one end rises a platform of heroic size on which figures of a heroic mold shall move. The scene shall be such as the world shows us, not as our own particular little street shows us. The movements of these scenes shall be noble and great: all shall be illuminated by a light such as the spheres give us, not such as the footlights give us, but such as we dream of."

MacKaye had a family tradition to urge him towards large experiments. His father, Steele MacKaye, irritated no doubt by the limitations of the nineteenth century theater as we are irritated by the limitations of the theater of the twentieth century, conceived and all but launched a grandiose and extraordinary scheme for a playhouse at the Chicago World's Fair. The Spectatorium, which was to seat ten thousand people and give a spectacle of music and drama, movement and light, dancing and action, on land and on water, was burned, however, before it could be completed.

The dominating idea in the younger MacKaye was to create a dramatic form of and for the people. It was to celebrate the works of humanity; *The Masque of St. Louis* commemorated the founding of the western city, and *Caliban* the tercentenary of Shakespeare's death. The MacKaye masque was to be acted and danced by the community with the assistance of a few trained players, and it was to be seen by as many as possible; in St. Louis 7,000 took part and 200,000 looked on. The experience of these community masques led MacKaye to want the active participation of the citizens as audience as well as of the citizens as actors, and in *The Evergreen Tree* he arranged a Christmas festival, to be given either out of doors or within, in which the spectators sang with the chorus and the actors, who passed through the midst of them. Another desire of MacKaye's was the enlarging of the characters of his masques to gigantic size. He did this literally in *The Masque of St. Louis* with the huge figure which stood for Cahokia. In *The Will of Song*, given its first production indoors, he began to work upon the idea of the "group being," a single dramatic entity visualized through a mass of players.

161

Whether or not Reinhardt began his first great circus-production, Sophocles' *Œdipus Rex*, with an esthetic philosophy, he had one before he was finished with *Orestes*, Hauptmann's *Festspiel*, and *Everyman*, the productions which followed. This was visible in his works as well as in the out-givings of his *Blätter des Deutschen Theaters*.

Like MacKaye, Reinhardt found a tremendous fascination in the relationship of this sort of production to man in the mass. In the "theater of the five thousand," as he called it, audiences are no longer audiences. They are the people. "Their emotions are simple and primitive, but great and powerful, as becomes the eternal human race." This follows from the nature of the theater and the relation of the actors to the audience. Monumentality is the key note of such great spaces. It is only the strongest and deepest feelings—the eternal elements—that can move these great gatherings. The small and the petty disappear.

Yet the emotion is direct and poignant, according to Reinhardt, because of a spiritual intimacy established by the new relation of actors and audience. In the Circus Schumann in Berlin Reinhardt revived the Greek orchestra. At one end of the building was the front of a temple. The actors came out in great mobs before the temple, upon an acting floor surrounded on three sides by banks of spectators. In the theory and the practice of Reinhardt there should be no curtain to conceal the setting. When the spectator enters he finds himself in the midst of great spaces, confronted by the whole scene, and himself a part of it. When he is seated and the play begins he finds that "the chorus rises and moves in the midst of the audience; the characters meet each other amid the spectators; from all sides the hearer is being impressed, so that gradually he becomes part of the whole, and is rapidly absorbed in the action, a member of the chorus, so to speak." This is a point that Reinhardt has always stressed in his big productions. This desire to make the spectators feel themselves participants is the same desire that MacKaye has carried to the point of actually making them so.

Reinhardt stressed the importance of the actors being made one with the audience through appearing in their midst. This maintained the intimacy which, he felt, was the most valuable contribution of the realistic movement in the theater—an intimacy produced in the main by the small auditoriums required if conversational acting were to be audible. Gigantic conceptions and tremendous emotional emphasis could thus be brought home to the spectator.

Technically the circus-theater made interesting demands. From the *régisseur* and the scene designer it required the utmost simplicity. Only the biggest and severest forms could be used. Light was the main source of decoration; it emphasized the important and hid the unessential. Acting, too, under-

163

went the same test. The player had to develop a simple and tremendous power. He had to dominate by intensity and by dignity, by the vital and the great. There had to be music in him, as there had to be music in the action itself.

The war prevented Reinhardt from continuing his experiments in mass-production, and bringing them to fruition in a theater built especially for the purpose. With the coming of peace he was able to remodel and re-open the old Circus Schumann as the Grosses Schauspielhaus. But in less than two years Reinhardt had left it in discouragement, his great dream shattered. By the summer of 1922 it could definitely be stamped an artistic failure—crowded to the doors every night.

It is not easy to trace the cause of failure, but it seems to lie in the curious fact that here Reinhardt was both careless and too careful. Physically the theater was wrong, if the theory was right, and its physical mistakes can be traced to Reinhardt. He was too careful in planning it and not courageous enough. Because he feared for its future as a financial undertaking, he seems to have compromised it in form, in order that it could be used as an ordinary, though huge playhouse if it failed as a new kind of theater. He put in the Greek orchestra surrounded on three sides by spectators. He made the floor flexible in its levels, and led it up by adjustable platforms to a stage at one side of the house. This much was right enough.

164

An impression of the Grosses Schauspielhaus in
Berlin. In the center rises the great dome, dimly
lit. At the left of the picture the looming shadow
of the hood above the forestage. A shaft of light
from the dome strikes across the space to the figure
of Judith, standing lonely and brave. Beyond,
row after row of faces just visible in the darkness.

But then he made the thing a compromise between the Greek theater, a circus, and the modern playhouse, by slapping a proscenium arch into the side wall and installing behind it a huge stage with all the mechanical folderols of the day—great dome, cloud-machine, revolving stage.   It was beyond human nature to resist the temptation of playing with the whole gigantic toy.   Neither Reinhardt nor the directors who succeeded him could be content, as they should have been, to lower the curtain across the proscenium, to plaster up the fourth wall. Perhaps there were not enough great dramas like *Œdipus* to draw for months the gigantic audiences needed to support the venture; but this only meant that such a theater must be maintained for festival performances, not that it must be filled with bastard productions requiring a picture stage and largely inaudible across the spaces of the Grosses Schauspielhaus.

Reinhardt was as careless in his selection of an architect as he was careful in compromise.   His original conception of the place was excellent.   He wanted it primitive and grand.   He wanted it to soar.   And he thought of early Gothic.   Between the pillars that had to be there to support the roof of the old circus, he wanted a dark blue background, a background of emptiness.   The dome over the middle was to vanish into a deep presence, lit sometimes by dim stars.   Some one got to Reinhardt, and persuaded him that he must be "modern;" he must assume a leadership in architecture; he must give a chance

165

to the greatest of the new architects, Hans Poelzig. Reinhardt consented. And Poelzig produced a very strange affair.

Some of the mistakes of the Grosses Schauspielhaus may be laid to the old building. The banks of seats are rather close against the roof, while the middle of the house is bridged by a gigantic dome. These conditions might have been minimized by giving the low portion lines that seemed to mount, and perhaps by closing in a large part of the dome or darkening it. Instead Poelzig has made the dome the only lovely and aspiring part of the architecture. It is a dream of soaring circles. If the building could only be turned upside down, and the actors could play in this flashing bowl, while the audience looked down upon them——!

The whole house, its innumerable corridors, its foyers and promenades, the walls of the auditorium, the ceiling, the capitals of the columns that support the dome, the dome itself —every inch of the whole is dominated by a single decorative *motif*, a very shoddy, cheap *motif*. This is a pendant, stalactite arch, borrowed from the Moorish architecture of Spain, and reduced to the lowest terms of mechanical rudeness. The theater is of concrete and stucco, and this dull shape is repeated endlessly and tediously, as if it had been scalloped out by a machine. Only in the dome, or when it is no more than hinted at in certain wall surfaces, does this shape do anything but bore and depress. On top of this, Poelzig had stained the

166

walls of many corridors and rooms in a yawping red, and turned the main foyer into a ghastly sea-green cavern. The theater is nervous, horrific, clangorous, glowering. There is nothing fountain-like. No spirit wells up in beauty. There is no dignity and no glory.

The fault may not be Poelzig's, but the lighting of the stage and orchestra seems unfortunately handled. Some of the lights for the inner stage are placed in front of the arch of the proscenium instead of behind it, and thus they illuminate it, and emphasize something that ought not to be there at all, let alone pointed out. The lights for the orchestra originally came wholly from the lower edge of the dome. It was necessary, however, to supply more, and they have been placed in an ugly red hood, which sticks out from the proscenium with no relation to the rest of the house. The lights in the dome stab with a glorious brilliance; the great beams seem to descend unendingly before they reach the tiny figures of the actors, and spot them out of the darkness. But these lights make the first mistake of trying to hide themselves, and the second mistake of not succeeding in doing so. How much better it would be if they were treated frankly as part of the theater; if their source were admitted; if these lamps were hung in great formal chandeliers made a part of the decorative design of the production. For Romain Rolland's *Danton* the astute Ernst Stern hung huge lanterns over the scene of the revolutionary

167

tribunal; it was a method that should have been perpetuated.

The productions that Reinhardt made are no longer to be seen in the Grosses Schauspielhaus, for repertory vanished from his theaters along with Reinhardt. You hear, however, of many interesting and beautiful things in *Danton*, in *Œdipus*, in *Hamlet*, in *Julius Cæsar*, in Hauptmann's *Florian Geyer*. But you see no such things now, or at least we did not see them when we were in Berlin. We saw the orchestra filled with seats—perhaps to swell the meager seating capacity of three thousand which was all Poelzig could include after he had wasted front space on rows of boxes and wide-spaced chairs, and perhaps because the new directors feared to use that glorious and terrible playing floor. We saw the forestage shrunk to a platform jutting out perhaps twenty feet. We saw a tedious performance of *Die Versunkene Glocke*, with the action shoved into the realistic proscenium, with the scenic artist fooling about with sloppily expressionist forms, and with the mountain spirit hopping down the hillside with a resounding wooden thump. We saw Hebbel's *Judith* done with much more effectiveness, though without real daring or vision.

Judith, however, shows some of the possibilities of such a theater. The beginning strikes in on the imagination with the impact of the shaft of light that beats down on Holofernes, sitting like some idol on his throne. Though he is almost back to the curtain line, instead of out in the midst of the people, he

168

The Inner Stage of the Grosses Schauspielhaus as set for the gates of Holofernes' palace. Designed by Ernst Schütte.

drives home the effect of seeing life in the round which such a theater can give. Here is talking sculpture. The costumer, as well as the actor, is given a new problem: the problem of clothes and the body that, like a statue, must mean something from every angle, must have beauty and significance from the back as much as from the front. The costume of Holofernes, at least, achieved this. The actor has another problem, the problem of a different movement and a different speech, movement slower and grander, or else long and swift, speech that is more sonorous, more elaborately spaced. The actor's part—in spite of rather second-rate players—is the part best done at the Grosses Schauspielhaus. There is a natural aptitude in the German player for the grand, slow speech, the roaring tempest. It is like the aptitude of the German people for the grand slow play. They like drive, rather than speed. They want to hear dull sonorous platitudes driven out by sheer belly-muscle.

There is one thing very beautiful in *Judith* and in this theater. It is the way a player can come forward to the edge of the forestage, and stand there alone, stabbed at by a great white light, surrounded first by emptiness, and beyond that by crowds, a brave figure alone in a great dim space. That is something you cannot feel in the chummy confines of a picture-frame.

The Grosses Schauspielhaus is a gigantic failure if you look at it with vision—and also a great portent. The place is ugly, and its purpose now debased, yet it hints at how beautiful a great, formal theater could be, how moving and inspiring its drama. Even in the wreckage, the idea still lives.

And if you try to bring a little of that same vision to the spectacle of the man who made this failure, and who ran away, you cannot deny an admiration for the courage to give up, to admit defeat, and then to go to the church, and to try to do there, in the sanctified birthplace of the modern theater, something to lift the spirit as high as the theater of the five thousand was to have lifted it.

CHAPTER XIV

THE THEATER OF THE THREE HUNDRED

SIZE is no mania with the French. They do not insist on buildings that are taller than those of any other nation, an empire that is larger, ambitions and dreams mightier and more terrible. So perhaps it was only natural that when a Frenchman wanted to present actors in a new relationship to their audience, he should choose for his theater a little hall in the Street of the Old Dovecot instead of a circus or a park.

Doubtless there were many reasons why Jacques Copeau's theater had to be small. A potent one may have been economy, a thing that accounts for the little theater movement far more than any theories of intimacy. The question of repertory also may have had weight. There are many sizes of drama, and there are special repertories for special theaters; but many more plays are possible for a theater of five hundred seats than for a theater of five thousand. *The Trojan Women* can be played to one hundred and twenty-nine people in the Toy Theater of Boston, as Maurice Browne proved; but *Le Misanthrope* is impossible in the Yale Bowl.

171

Copeau's theater had to be small, not only because he had little money and a great love of all sorts of plays, but also because—and this counted more than even the French liking for the moderate and the exact—the thing he was interested in was the actor and not a grandiose idea. He ended by creating the first presentational playhouse in the modern world, by maintaining for a long time the most radical, and by achieving after some years the most successful. But he began by looking for some place for his actors to act. They were to be a company of fresh, sensitive, intelligent spirits bringing an intense and honest art to those who might care for it. Copeau had found his actors in all manner of places besides the routine theaters. He had talked to them about everything but make-up, curtain calls, and how to be natural on the stage. He had played with them and worked with them in the country, rehearsing the first pieces of the repertory in a barn. He did not intend to dump them down into one of the ordinary theaters of Paris. Copeau proposed to take the hall that his resources permitted, and to make it over to suit the spirit of his company. He could build no ideal theater, but he could make one in which his actors would escape the realisms and the pretenses of the modern theater, and would play to and with the audience as their spirit demanded.

And so we have the Théâter du Vieux-Colombier. It is not at all like the hideous theater-hall that was there before. It is not quite as it was when Copeau clòsed his first season before the war. It is not in the least like the Garrick Theater, which he remade in New York in 1917; as a matter of fact it is not so good. It is not very charming in its shape or its decorations, and Copeau is as careless as Reinhardt about things like good painting and clean walls. But this Vieux-Colombier is a distinguished and a jolly place all the same, the happiest and the healthiest theater west of Vienna.

It is hard to know where to begin a description of this curious playhouse. Suppose you had never been to the Vieux-Colombier, but suppose you knew that this was a theater without the illusion of Realism, and suppose you sought for the thing that would tell you this the quickest. What would you see? Probably the steps that lead from the stage to the forestage, and even from the forestage to the seats of the audience. There are no footlights, and so you have the pleasure of seeing the square, firm edge where the stage floor ends. This edge bends into a large curve in the middle, with three curved steps below, and it angles out at the sides to where smaller steps join those of the middle on an ample forestage. These steps and the edge of the stage do more than any one thing in the theater to signal that you are not looking into a picture-frame. Even when they are not used, as in *Les Frères Karamazov*, these steps keep you warily alive to that fact.

When you examine the theater more closely you discover that

173

there is no proscenium. The nearest thing to it is the last of the arches which hold up the roof of the auditorium. There is a curtain, to be sure, but it does not fall behind pillars, and it does not cover the forestage. It descends at that point where the walls of the auditorium become the walls of the stage, and it merely serves to hide one end of this long room while the stage hands make small changes in the permanent setting.

The permanent setting, like the theater itself, is an experimental product of the attempt to provide what the actors need. It is really no more than a balcony placed against the back wall, with an arched opening in the middle, and with walls at the sides that let the actors, who have gone out through the arch, get off stage unseen. This balcony is so solidly built that it cannot be taken out, but certain portions are alterable. The changes in setting are managed by changing the width of the arch or the line of the top of the balcony, by adding doors, steps at one side, or railings, and particularly by placing significant properties or screens upon the stage. Louis Jouvet, stage director as well as Copeau's best actor, has done many ingenious things to make his settings varied enough and characteristic enough without losing the permanent thing that is common to them all, and that aids in banishing realistic illusion. A detail that shows the working of his mind is to be found in the screens that he uses to create a room in *Les Frères Karamazov;* by giving them two or three inches of thickness and a certain

Les Frères Karamazov: the Gypsy Inn. This
sketch and the following one show the permanent skeleton-setting of Copeau's Théâtre du
Vieux-Colombier in Paris. Here, in an arrangement of paneled screens Louis Jouvet has caught
the mood of the scene without reference to details of "atmosphere."

amount of molding, he has escaped the impression of the bare, the unsubstantial, and the untheatrical which the screens of other designers produce.

The balcony is a most useful feature. It was not accident that put a balcony in the Elizabethan theater or made the Greeks use the theologium. It serves a practical purpose, of course, in any scheme of permanent setting, for it makes it unnecessary to build balconies for scenes that especially call for them. A good deal more important to the director is the movement up and down, as well as sideways and back and forth, which it gives him. With the forestage, the main stage, and the balcony, Copeau has almost as useful a base for composing action in three dimensions as Jessner has in the steps which he uses in various productions in Berlin.

Sheldon Cheney has called Copeau's stage a "naked stage." It is a happy accident of language that, when you call it a concrete stage, you describe the material of which it is made and the feeling of sharp, definite statement which resides in everything done upon it. The wall at the right of the audience is solid, the wall at the back, too; the ceiling of the stage has some openings between steel girders, but it is more like the floor than the "flies" of the average theater. Only in the left wall of the stage are there any openings. Through these the actors manage to exit into the next building. The floor of the stage, except at the edges, is even more adamant. It will not yield to

175

pleas for atmosphere, illusion or any of the gewgaws of our theater. It is solid concrete. Copeau wanted to give the actor's feet a sense of support which they cannot get from yielding and resounding wood. At the sides is a small section in timber which permits the use of a stairway to a lower room as in *The S. S. Tenacity* or *Les Frères Karamazov.* In the forestage are two other openings, covered by· wooden and concrete slabs.

Jouvet's lighting system is ingenious and philosophically sound, if not altogether perfect. Practically all the light comes from four large lamps hung in the auditorium. They replace footlights, borderlights, and floods from the sides. Illumination from the auditorium itself is essential to good stage lighting; the footlights are an unhappy makeshift. David Belasco very wisely uses a battery of lamps hidden in the face of the first balcony. In German theaters, the huge 6000-candlepower bulbs developed since the war, tempt directors to inefficient and distracting lighting from the ventilator above the main chandelier in the roof of the auditorium. Neither the latter method nor Belasco's is wholly satisfactory in a theater that forswears representation, a theater like the Grosses Schauspielhaus or the Vieux-Colombier or the Redoutensaal in Vienna. Electric light on the stage begins as an imitation of the real. If a table is illuminated by a large light in the first border, there must be a lamp above the table in such a position as to suggest that it is doing all the work. The next step is to use light for illumination and composition—for beauty, in fact—without bothering to try to make it seem to come from some natural source in the setting. When such light comes from the auditorium we may get composition, but we also get a throw-back to the source of the light itself. The ray carries our eye up to some lens-lamp trying unsuccessfully to hide in the bottom of the dome of the Grosses Schauspielhaus, or in the top of the ceiling of the Burgtheater. A new problem arises. It should be answered by making the source frankly visible. The hoods themselves of large bulbs have a shape that would make them interesting and not without significance in the Grosses Schauspielhaus; or a new shape could be supplied to harmonize with architecture or setting. In the Redoutensaal we find glorious old crystal chandeliers lighting the stage—an accidental result of the fact that the Viennese government converted Maria Theresa's ballroom into a playhouse. In the Vieux-Colombier Jouvet makes no bones about admitting where his light is coming from. He places the bulbs in octagonal lanterns, which, by revolving on an axis, present different colored sides for the light to pass through; the lanterns may also be moved in such directions as to throw the light upon any desired part of the stage. These lanterns are frankly visible; and, though they are not a pleasing shape, they fit esthetically with the theory of this theater. Here is electric lighting presented at last as the thing it really is, not as an imitation of something else.

The greatest faults of the Vieux-Colombier over which Copeau had control, and which he could easily have avoided, lie in the color and quality of painting on the stage. The concrete and the cream of the auditorium take warm lights; but in portions of the stage itself, Copeau has used a cold gray that is surely unfortunate. Much that you see is shoddy. If the paint chips off a corner, nobody bothers to replace it. Rivet heads and structural iron show when they have no relation to the shapes on the stage. Now it is a good thing not to spend too much energy on the physical side of the theater, but there is a difference between austerity and slovenliness.

Actual productions, animated by the actors and graced with some of Jouvet's scenic arrangements, do a great deal to make the stage wholly attractive. *The S. S. Tenacity*, a realistic play with a French café for its setting, makes interesting demands on this non-realistic stage. The demands are met, and met successfully. There is a counter at one side with racks for bottles, a wooden door in the arch at the back, a table in the center, and above it—the mark of Realism—a shaded lamp, from which a great deal of the stage light comes. With the actors giving us the sense of French life which was missing in the New York and Viennese productions, we have here a performance which might almost be enclosed in a proscenium frame. But there is in the acting, as in the setting, much that is non-realistic, much that seems representational only by contrast with the dominating spirit and physique of the theater and its people.

In the playlet that goes with *The S. S. Tenacity*, Mérimée's *Le Carrosse du St.-Sacrement*, we are back in a piece from the romantic period, a comedy of clear and artificial vigor. A screen and some hangings with a southern flash to them set the stage for eighteenth-century Peru. Copeau himself has the same Punch-like visage that he presents to you in his own study, but now he manages to make you think him a Spanish puppet, an exasperated and wily doll. The same Punch appears in *Les Frères Karamazov*, but a Punch of the intellect, a tragic marionette dangling on the strings of rationalism. At the end, when Ivan goes mad, you may see most clearly the subtle exaggeration which is at the heart of the acting of Copeau's company. The whirling body, the legs that beat a crazy tattoo on the floor, the twisting head and the boggling eyes, are none of them copied from a candidate for the asylum. They are all an explanation of what sort of lines in the figure of a crazy man would strike the imagination, what angles and movements would most sharply indicate lunacy.

Karamazov is effectively composed on this stage by a few draperies for the first scene, a line of curtains hiding the whole stage and begging the question in the second scene, a flight of steps for the hall of the Karamazovs, and two heavy screens for the inn. There is nothing so fine as the interminable steps that lead up from the balcony at the Garrick to the wretched room of Smerdiakov; but there is enough improvement in the very excellent acting seen in New York, to make up for this. Jouvet's father is gigantically good; set beside his Aguecheek, it puts this young man among the most interesting actors of Europe. Paul Œttly, as the eldest brother, plays the striking scene in the inn of the gypsies with uncommon vigor, and the stage direction sweeps the scene along to a burning climax. The intensity of the actors in this play, added to the intensity of the play itself, demonstrates how completely a formal theater of this kind, and a type of acting which is a reasoned sort of explanation, rather than a thing of life or of acting, can stand up beside the Realism of our directors when it is at its best.

In *Twelfth Night* you find the company clear out of the shackles of realistic or semi-realistic plays, and happy in the beautiful playhouse of fantasy. And here the quality of exposition—which you may trace back to Copeau's profession of critic, and forward through the days given to the reading and study and analysis of each new play—has almost altogether disappeared. The playing is spontaneous, or it is nothing. Suzanne Bing's Viola is a-quiver with radiance and wonder. Jean Le Goff's Orsino is no such God-favored performance, but

La Carrosse du Saint-Sacrement at the *Vieux-Colombier:* another arrangement of Copeau's permanent setting.

his eyes are lit with an ecstasy of love-sickness. The comedians are far from Englishmen; but their creations are immensely funny: Jouvet's gently gawking Aguecheek, Romain Bouquet's shaven-headed, almost Oriental Sir Toby, Robert Allard's extraordinary clown, the finest either of us had ever seen. It is interesting, for once, to see Malvolio put in his place as a character, and not given the star's spotlight to preen in; it might be a more satisfactory arrangement if Albert Savry could be funnier in his dry Puritanism.

Twelfth Night triumphs at the Vieux-Colombier by virtue of the spirit of the actors, and the vision of the director. The costuming is bad—an unsuccessful attempt to make Illyria, as it might well be, a land of no time or place but Poetry; and the setting is no more than bright and freakish in a Greenwich Village way. But in the costumes and up and down the setting these players frisk, weaving patterns of beauty and fun that link them into the true spirit of the play. The curtain is there at convenient times to make the forestage into a neutral zone for duke or sea captain, and between this forestage and the balconied space behind there is room for all of Shakespeare's play to race along just as he wrote it. With the trap door in the forestage to act as cellar, Malvolio can be incarcerated belowstairs and happily out of sight—much as Shakespeare intended.

Copeau is a believer in gymnastics. (He is also a believer in improvisation, a school of playwrights, and other things

181

whose absence makes him grow impatient with his theater). Through months and years of strenuous labor, he is training half a dozen young people of his own school to have bodies that are as well under control as a gymnast's. The performances of the Vieux-Colombier draw on players not so well trained, but they show what physical command can accomplish. Here you see acting that makes you think again of sculpture and its relation to the new theater.

Copeau's people can meet the test which the theater with a Greek orchestra, like the Grosses Schauspielhaus, exacts. They can play "in the round." Their bodies can be seen from all sides, and still keep expressiveness and beauty. They have learned to master their bodies, as well as their voices, and they are able to make the lines of arms and torsos and knees speak directly to the audience. When Jouvet sharply underlines and almost caricatures the salient shape of old Karamazov he is able to escape from ordinary representation, which may or may not make its point, and he is able to push his conception of the wicked, vital old man into almost direct physical contact with the audience. I have often wondered when the actor would learn the lesson of sculpture. There were centuries of almost literal representation, with the inner expression of the artist and the artist's sense of Form struggling furiously to impose itself upon Reality, and failing more often than succeeding. Then, with Rodin came the sense that sculpture could make representation a distinctly secondary matter. There could be expression first, and resemblance afterwards, if at all. Idea, which is one sort of Form, enters the clay with Stanislas Szukalsky. Expression and idea, poised in the human body, begin to inform acting directly and openly in the company of the Vieux-Colombier. The first presentational theater adds the medium of the body to the medium of the voice.

CHAPTER XV

THE REDOUTENSAAL—A PLAYHOUSE OF PERMANENCE

IN Vienna on Christmas Day, 1921, there were no matches in the match-stands of the cafés and no paper in the hotel writing rooms. Some of the well-to-do and the recklessly soft-hearted had begun to feel that they could afford to keep pet dogs again; but there were no silk stockings on those most un-Teuton ankles that paraded the Burgring. You may guess, therefore, that there was no butter on the tables of the middle classes, and no milk in the houses of those who, by a curious clairvoyance of language, are called the working people.

Two nights later three or four hundred citizens, with bits of bread and meat wrapped in paper and stowed in their pockets, could be seen seated in a great and splendid ballroom of Maria Theresa's palace, under the light of crystal chandeliers and the glow of priceless Gobelins, watching the first performance, *The Marriage of Figaro*, in a theater a stride ahead of any in Europe.

They had paid good money at one of the doors of that extraordinary old building, the Hofburg, which rambles from the

184

Opera to the Burgtheater half across the shopping district of
Vienna. After they had parted from two or three thousand
crowns apiece, they had wound up stone stairways between
white walls and twists of old ironwork, passed through cloak-
rooms where princesses once left their wraps, and a supper room
where artists may cheerfully go mad over molding, pediment
and mirror, and reached at last the Theater in dem Redoutensaal. They found one of the handsomest baroque rooms in Europe holding within its beauty both a stage and an auditorium.
A row of Gobelin tapestries filled the lower reaches of the walls.
Above were moldings and pilasters, cornices and pargeting,
spandrels and pediments, fillets and panelling, an ordered richness of ornament that held suspended in its gray and golden
haze mirrors that echoed beauty, and chandeliers radiant with
light. At one end of the room, beneath great doors and a balcony which the architect had planned in 1744, was a new structure; it broke the line of the Gobelins, but continued the panelling, freshened to cream and gold, in a curving wall across a
platform and in double stairs leading to the balcony. With
man's unfailing instinct for the essence of life, the audience
promptly identified this roofless shell as a stage. There was a
platform, of course, but there was no proscenium. There were
doors and windows in the curving wall, but no woodwings,
borders, flats, or backdrops. There was even a something along
the front of the platform which might conceal footlights, but

there was nothing to be seen that looked more like scenery than a row of screens.

Such is the room in which the forces of the Austrian State Opera House have been giving *The Marriage of Figaro* and *The Barber of Seville*, and in which Reinhardt began late in 1922 the most interesting experiment of his most experimental life—the presentation of plays under a unique condition of theatrical intimacy between actor and audience.

It is an odd spectacle, this of Vienna, the bankrupt, going lightheartedly out on the most advanced experiment in production yet attempted in Europe. One of its oddest angles is that the man who made an empress's ballroom over into a theater is a socialist—President Vetter of the Staatstheaterverwaltung, the bureau under the republic which controls the State playhouses. The conversion was not an easy matter. Opponents rose up inside the State theaters and outside them. Vienna was engaged for months upon one of those artistic quarrels from which it is always drawing new health and spirit.

When President Vetter had won his point he plunged briskly ahead at the work of making over the ballroom into a very special kind of theater without marring its beauty. Part of the old balcony came out, mirrors replaced doors and windows down the sides of the hall, and Oberbaurat Sebastien Heinrich set to work on the problem of creating a permanent architectural setting for the stage which should harmonize with the

186

The Redoutensaal in Vienna as arranged for the
first scene of *The Marriage of Figaro*. The
room called for in the text is indicated by a row
of crimson screens set straight across the stage and
pierced in the center by a door. In the scheme of
production indicated by this unique environment
such a mere indication is sufficient to establish
setting and mood.

lovely room, yet stand out from it significantly enough to center attention on the acting space. Meantime President Vetter took another look at the Gobelins which had satisfied Maria Theresa, and decided that they weren't quite good enough; others had to be found. Even now he is a little doubtful about those on the right hand wall.

The work of the Oberbaurat is admirable. He has continued the molding above the Gobelins, and made it the top of the curving wall which is the background for the stage. This shell is broken at each side by a casement, which holds either a door or a window, and two masked openings. Through one of these, close to the front of the stage, a curtain the height of the wall is run out to hide changes in the screens and furniture upon the stage. At the back, where the shell curves close to the old balcony of the ballroom, the State architect has placed a pair of graceful steps, which meet at the top, and provide, underneath, an exit to the rear. For lighting, there are the foots in their unobtrusive trough, and small floods placed in the gap where the curtain moves; but by far the larger part of the illumination comes from the seven chandeliers in the ceiling of the hall. The chandeliers towards the rear are sometimes turned half down or even off, but essentially it is the same light which illumines both players and audience.

This light and the formal and permanent character of the stage stamp the Redoutensaal with a character as old as it is fresh. This theater goes beyond Copeau's Vieux-Colombier in the attempt to re-establish in our century that active relationship between actor and spectator which existed in the great theaters of other centuries, and towards which the finest minds of the theater have been striving. Here is a stage freed from all the associations of modern stage-setting, innocent of machinery or illusions, essentially theatrical. Actors must be actors upon its boards. They cannot try to represent actual people; they can only present themselves to the audience as artists who will give them a vision of reality.

This is comparatively easy in opera. There is no realistic illusion about a valet who sings a soliloquy on his master's more intimate habits. People who quarrel in verse to a merry tune are most unlikely to be mistaken for the neighbors next door. With music and the stage of the Redoutensaal to aid them, the singers of the State Opera manage to give a roughly presentational performance. In direction there is nothing notable to be seen, unless it is the wedding scene of *Figaro* with the Count striding up and down across the front of the stage, opposed in figure and in action to the plaguing women above upon the stairs. The acting possibilities of this stage, however, are very great. Reinhardt saw them vividly in the summer of 1922, while he was makng preparations for his five productions in September: *Turandot* by Gozzi, *Stella* and *Clavigor* by Goethe, *Le Misanthrope* by Molière, and *Dame Cobalt* by Calderon.

188

He saw the possibilities and the difficulties of acting also, and he rejoiced that he was to have old and tried associates like Moissi, Pallenberg and Krauss with him once more when he began his experiment with a theater far more exacting than the Grosses Schauspielhaus, and a technique of acting very hard to regain after so many years of Realism.

So far as there must be indications of time and place upon this stage, a beginning in experiment has been made. It has not been a particularly good beginning, but it shows the opportunities for the artist, and also the limitations. They are very nearly identical. It is the business of the scene designer who works here to draw from the Redoutensaal itself the *motifs* and colors which he shall add to the permanent setting. It is his privilege, using only these things, to give the scene just the fillip of interest which the play demands.

Alfred Roller, a veteran of the scenic revolt of fifteen years ago, and, next to Reinhardt's artist, Ernst Stern, the most distinguished German scenic designer of his time, has made the screens and set pieces for *The Marriage of Figaro* and *The Barber of Seville*. There is little or no good to be said of his work in the latter piece. The screens with which he indicates a room in the first act, and the bulky gate which he sets down across the stairs in the second act, are bad as to color, and quite at odds with the Redoutensaal. Obviously he could have made so much more amusing a gate out of the permanent stairs, and given his scene a Spanish stamp by a circle of vivid, tight-packed flowers in the center. *The Marriage of Figaro* is much better, though here again Roller could have done far better if he had turned his eyes up to the walls above him. The first scene, the servant's room, is made by a row of antique screens of faded crimson placed well down stage. Through a door in the central one, you see green screens, which, in the second scene are to define the room of the wife. With an excellent sense of climax, Roller proceeds from the shallow stage of the first scene to the deeper stage of the second, and finally sweeps in the whole permanent setting for the wedding in the third scene. More than that, he calls the stairs and balcony into play, and finally opens the great doors above the balcony to let us see beyond to a room of crimson hangings and more crystal. The last scene, the garden, is shoddily conceived, with a few uninteresting potted trees, a bad painting of Schönbrunn in the exit under the steps, and a sickly attempt at moonlight from the floodlights and foots. Why not, you wonder, delicate, artificial, gilded hedges along the walls, and fruit trees flattened on *espaliers* against the steps?

Unquestionably the lighting problem in the Redoutensaal is not yet solved. Reinhardt looks to solve it with a large light or two concealed in the forward chandeliers. This may make the illumination of the stage a little more flexible and expressive; but it is quite as likely that the way to light the stage is

The first scene of *The Barber of Seville* as given in the Redoutensaal. A not altogether successful attempt by Professor Roller to create an architectural unit which should suggest a Spanish exterior while harmonizing with the decorations of the ballroom.

without the least pretense at illusion. At any rate footlights and lights from the side are distressing reminders of the conventional theater.

Almost as reminiscent is the curtain which slides out between acts while the stage hands move the screens. Why a curtain at all—unless the curtain of darkness? Why not uniformed attendants managing the simple matter of screens or small set pieces with the aplomb of actors? Or if there must be a curtain, why a crimson sheet; why not a hanging whose folds continue the *motif* of the Gobelins at each side?

Perhaps the most serious question concerned with the physical arrangements of this stage is whether there should not be some scheme of levels other than floor and balcony. A lower forestage would aid the director in composing his people, and getting movement and variety out of this fixed and therefore limited setting. It would also aid an audience that is seated almost on a flat floor.

The sceptic may find other limitations in the Redoutensaal. And he will be right if he points out that its atmosphere is too sharply artificial in its distinction to permit every sort of play to be given here. Gorky's *Night Lodging* might be played in the Redoutensaal as a literally tremendous *tour de force*, but it would be in the face of spiritual war between the background of the stage and the physical horrors of the slums which the play describes. Plays for the Redoutensaal must have some quality of distinction about them, a great, clear emotion free from the bonds of physical detail, a fantasy or a poetry as shining as crystal, some artificiality of mood, or else an agreement in period with the baroque. You can imagine Racine or Corneille done perfectly here, Euripides only by great genius, *The Weavers* not at all. Nothing could suit Molière better, or Beaumarchais or the Restoration dramatists. Shakespeare could contribute *Twelfth Night* and *A Midsummer Night's Dream*, perhaps *Romeo and Juliet*, but never *Hamlet*. Here, of course, is a perfect stage for Oscar Wilde, a good stage for Somerset Maugham, A. A. Milne, some of Clare Kummer. The Moscow Art Theater would have no trouble with *The Cherry Orchard*. More or less at random, you think of Bahr's *Josephine*, *The School for Scandal*, *The Sabine Women*, *Lysistrata*, *The Mollusc*, *A Marriage of Convenience*, *The Truth*, *Prunella*, *The Beggar's Opera*. The one impossible barrier to performance in the Redoutensaal is Atmosphere. If a play is drenched in the emotions of firesides, poppy fields, moonlit gardens or natural physical things, it is impossible here.

These are the limitations of the Redoutensaal, not of its idea. The permanent setting and its enclosing hall can take the shapes of other periods and meet almost every demand of the drama except atmosphere. Ideally the hall should have some sober yet arresting architecture common to many periods. A neutral order of this sort might be the blank Roman arches and plain pilasters which are seen so often in modern buildings. The chandeliers might take a form less ornate and less blazing; nuances of lighting, if desirable, might then be achieved. More important, however, would be to have three interchangeable shells and steps. One set of walls should be classical and severe, suited to Greek tragedy, *Julius Cæsar*, and, with a bit of brightening, to Shaw's *Cæsar and Cleopatra*. Another shell should strike the note of artificial distinction with which the Redoutensaal now echoes. The third should be of dark, paneled wood, to suit Shakespearean tragedy, the comedy of Goldsmith, and modern pieces from *Rosmersholm* to *Getting Married* and from *Alice Sit-by-the Fire* to *Magda*.

The idea of a permanent room in which to act a related repertory is thoroughly applicable even to our peepshow playhouses with their prosceniums. It would be possible to install a shell or room on the stage of any reasonably presentable theater, such as Henry Miller's, the Little, the Booth, the Plymouth, the Selwyn in New York, the Künstler in Munich, the Volksbühne, the Kammerspiele in Berlin, the Comédie des Champs-Elysées in Paris, St. Martin's in London. The room would have to be formal, probably without a ceiling, and certainly far more like a wall than a room. Such a compromise seems the only chance America may have of experimenting with the idea of the Redoutensaal. There is nowhere in this country a room so naturally fitted to the purpose by its beauty

193

as was the ballroom of the Hapsburgs. The building of a fresh structure is a little too much to ask; for we have hardly the directors or actors to launch unpractised upon such a costly and critical test. It might be risked perhaps, as Frank Lloyd Wright proposed risking it, in a theater of a purely artistic nature far from Broadway. Wright designed for Aline Barnsdall a playhouse to be erected in California, with an adjustable proscenium, a stage with a dome that all but continued over the auditorium, and, upon the stage, a plain curving wall some ten feet high, following the shape of the dome. The nearest analogy to the Redoutensaal that has been actually attempted in America is probably the adaptation which Director Sam Hume and the artists Rudolph Schaeffer and Norman Edwards made of the Greek Theater in Berkeley, California, for *Romeo and Juliet* and *Twelfth Night*. There is a certain significance, however, in the pleasure which our scenic artists seem to get out of a play which gives them only one setting to design, but which requires them to wring from it, by means of lights, many moods and a variety of visual impressions. Lee Simonson's circus greenroom for *He Who Gets Slapped* and Norman-Bel Geddes' sitting room for *The Truth About Blayds* showed how seductive to the artist of the theater may be the game of playing with lights in a permanent setting.

Approached purely from the point of view of scenic art, or the so-called new stagecraft, the Redoutensaal presents excel-

194

lent reasons for its existence. Historically it could be defended by a study of the theater from the Greeks, with their day-lit, architectural background, to Georgian times when the stage and the house were both lighted by the same chandeliers, and the wide apron, the boxes, and the proscenium made a sort of permanent setting which was varied by the shifting backcloths. But if we go no further back than the days when Craig and Appia were beginning to write, and before their voices and their pencils had won an audience among theater directors, we shall find the start of an evolutionary development for which the idea of the Redoutensaal provides a plausible climax. In the first decade of the twentieth century, the "flat" was flat indeed, and the painted wing and backdrop ruled. If there was any depth, it was the space between wing and wing, or the false space of painted perspective. Then the ideas of Craig and Appia, making a curious alliance with Realism, forced the plastic upon the stage. The solid, three-dimensional setting dominated. When directors and artists began to discover the physical and spiritual limitations of "real" settings which could present nothing bigger than the actual stage space, many went back to the painted flat. It was a different flat, however, one painted with dynamic and expressive design. The third method is seldom quite satisfactory. The living actor, with his three-dimensional being, clashes with the two-dimensional painting. The result is bad from a realistic or illusionistic

195

point of view; and, as soon as we think of the stage in terms of a frank convention, we find·that we want the emphasis thrown upon the actor as the more interesting and the more difficult element. We want a defined and permanent artificiality that shall give the actor scope, serve as a *pied-à-terre*, not join in a fantastic competition. We can escape plastic and limited reality in the Redoutensaal, while we supply the actor with a background that harmonizes with the living character of his body. At the same time we can secure the vivid indication of mood or time or place which we seek, and achieve it more vividly because of the permanence of the main fabric of the stage, and its contrast with the merely indicated setting.

German scene designers and directors move in theory steadily towards what they call the podium, the platform pure and simple, from which the player addresses the audience openly as a player. In practice they tend steadily to try to approach this by driving out as much of changing scenic background as possible. They place something in the middle of the stage, a table, a flight of steps, a pillar, a bed, and they try to eliminate the rest of the stage. Jessner does this in Berlin by using his cyclorama as a neutral boundary without character in itself. Fehling, the director of *Masse-Mensch*, uses black curtains, and the artist Krehan by the same means tries to center our attention on small set pieces placed in the middle of the stage and designed to represent corners of rooms or a sofa by a window.

196

THE REDOUTENSAAL

Black curtains appear everywhere in Germany—perhaps as an expression of the mood of the beaten nation, but also unquestionably from a desire to drive out both Realism and pretense and to leave as little as possible upon the stage except the actor and the barest and most essential indication of setting. The German uses black curtains to achieve nothingness. Instead he gets desolation, spiritual negation. In the Redoutensaal, the actor is backed up by space. It is a positive presence instead of a negative background. Yet it does not obtrude, this splendid room, with its gold and gray, its mirrors and its tapestries. These things float in the back of consciousness, filling what might be a disquieting void or a depressing darkness. Always the cream walls dominate the gray, and always the living actor, driving his message directly at the spectator, dominates them all.

CHAPTER XVI

THE CIRQUE MEDRANO

PERHAPS the gladiators gave it a bad name. At any rate for twenty centuries men have hesitated to put anything more serious than a clown or an athlete in the middle of an audience. The Romans could hardly be called a timorous, a sensitive or a conventional people, yet even they never thought of presenting a play in an amphitheater. C. Curio, rich and reckless, celebrated the death of his father by building two great wooden theaters back to back, giving performances in both at the same time, then whirling the spectators about on turn tables, until they faced each other, and the two semicircles of seats joined and made one huge arena. But, though Curio was reckless of money and of the lives of his guests, he was careful of the esthetic proprieties. The actors performed in the theaters, and the animals in the arena.

So far as the feelings of the Drama can be learned, she did not approve of the way the Romans shoved her actors out of the old Greek orchestra, and crammed them into a shallow little box, which they called a stage. The first chance that the Drama had, she climbed down close to the people again, and

198

played on the stone floor of the medieval churches. Even Shakespeare did not have the temerity to try to put her back in a box. It is said that there were rare times, as in some of the outdoor mysteries of the Middle Ages and while the pageant wagons carried the actors and their scenes into the squares of the English towns, when you might have found the Drama entirely surrounded by the hosts of her admirers. But some curious and perverse power seems to have schemed through the centuries to seize a decadent time like the Roman days or the last fifty years in modern Europe, and clap the Drama in a box. And to-day, when the Drama is bravely insisting on a little air and light, the power is still strong enough to keep the Drama's liberators from placing her naked and unashamed in the center of her fellows. She is no longer a peepshow lure, but we still hesitate to treat her as a goddess.

Occasionally a theorist, who is as sick as the rest of us of the fourth wall convention, comes forward with some extraordinary proposal to put the audience in the middle of the drama. Furttenbach in the seventeenth century laid out a square theater with a stage in each corner. Oskar Strnad of Vienna wants to place a doughnut stage two thirds round the audience; and some Frenchman has advocated whirling the doughnut. Anything to distract the spectator from the drama; nothing to concentrate him upon it.

In the "Theater of the Five Thousand" devised by Max

Reinhardt in Berlin, and in the imitation which Firmin Gémier launched at the Cirque d'Hiver in Paris, the audience and the drama at last met in the circus.   But for some curious reason— at which I have only guessed in a more or less absurd fashion— neither Reinhardt nor Gémier was courageous or far-seeing enough to use the circus as a circus.   Neither dared put the players in the center, and forget the old stage.   At one side there always lingered a palace or a proscenium.

Reinhardt might make the excuse that for such a scheme he needed a round circus, and that a round circus would be far too big for the drama.   (He would not be absurd enough to say that Moissi or Pallenberg could not act unless all the audience saw all his face all the time).   There are round circuses in Europe, however, and small, round circuses, and if Reinhardt could not find one in Berlin, he could have built one for half the money he put into reconstructing the Circus Schumann into the Grosses Schauspielhaus.

Up on Montmartre, just under the last heights on which perches Sacré Cœur, there is such a circus.   An intimate circus, a little circus, just the place to begin the last experiment with the theater.   Copeau could go straight there from the Vieux-Colombier, and throw his *Scapin* into the ring without a second's hesitation.   It would bowl over Paris and half the theatrical world.

Copeau could go straight there, but I think the audience

should be required, for a time, to make a detour *via* the top of Montmartre. Certainly that is the only way to approach the Cirque Medrano to-day. A *fiacre* to the funicular. The funicular to the base of the cathedral. A stroll all round that boarded-up curiosity. A look-off at Paris swimming in the ebb-tide of the summer sun. Then supper in the Place du Tertre. Not for the food, which is as good as any *cuisine bourgeoise;* nor for the trees and window-groups out of Manet; nor for the tubby widow of forty-five who sings:

Je le proclame,
Les mains de femme
Sont les bijoux
Dont je suis fou. . . .

or the ancient with the two brass buttons in the back of his surtout and the patience of an English politician, who recites inaudible and probably unintelligible poetry before passing the hat. Supper in the Place du Tertre is an appropriate prelude to the Cirque Medrano because of the dog that watches all evening from the tin roof of an impossibly ruined house, and the women straight out of the French Revolution, the days of '48 and the Commune, who stand about with their great naked arms akimbo, and their strong sharp chins, high cheek bones, and eagle eyes waiting for the liberty cap to crown them. The dog and the women, they are the audience and the show. They are the Cirque Medrano.

201

This circus is a golden bowl. At the bottom, no sawdust but a carpet of hemp, a great "welcome" doormat without the lettering; we take the deed for the word. Outside the ring is a parapet nicely carpeted in yellow; one of the clowns finds it amusing to roll round this track on his shoulders. Above the parapet rise steep rows of seats, half of them in bright orange for the spectators with fifty or sixty cents to spend. Higher up the thin and graceful pillars which support the roof cut across the vision a little; here there are only benches and the *dévotés*. At opposite sides of the ring, walled passages lead out to the greenroom and public entrances which circle underneath the seats. Exits for the audience pierce the rows at the four quarters. From the disk of the dome above, sixteen great lamps blaze down on the ring, and sometimes a spotlight or two punctuate the darkness.

If you like to take your pleasure sentimentally, a performance at the Cirque Medrano is like opening old letters—with a comic valentine now and then for tonic. Huck Finn saw a one-ring circus; but Gentry's Dog and Pony Show is the farthest that the present generation ever get from the three-ring-and-two-stage monstrosity which deafens our ears and dulls our eyes.

The Cirque Medrano is the proper place for artists and *connoisseurs*. The fifteen hundred people that it holds can study —and do study—with the minute intensity of an anatomical clinic, M. Grossi and Coquette, as the horseman, quite as proud as his mare, puts her through five minutes of marching to music. They turn their eyes with just as much appreciation to watch the aerialists, plunging into their dangerous pastimes under the lights. Here M. Lionel, *Roi du Vertige*, gets the sort of attention he could never win on the vaudeville stage; it must seem to him sometimes, as he manœuvers gingerly on a chair balanced by its right hind leg in the neck of a bottle which is perched in turn on a ten foot pole, that the towering rows of seats are about to topple over on the strange career which he has made of himself.

There is no question, then, about the sight-lines of the theater which Copeau should make out of the Cirque Medrano. There never was such an auditorium for sheer visibility. The last rows are better than the first; they take in the whole audience as well as the show, while all you can say for the front seats is that they would show you half of the laughing or crying crowd of men and women, hanging over the actors in far from mute adoration. The slant of these seats is greater than the slant in Max Littmann's theaters in Munich, but, because the rows swing all round, you never get that feeling of awful vacancy and gap which comes to spectators in the upper rows of the Prinzregenten and the Künstler Theaters in Munich. And there is no proscenium arch to press down upon the poor midgets at the bottom of the playhouse.

"But their backs?   How about the actors' backs?"

That is a foolish question from any one who has ever seen Copeau's players, who has watched Jouvet's back play the coarse, immense Karamazov, or seen his legs and buttocks send Aguecheek shuffling across the stage, or caught the whole quick poise of Suzanne Bing's Viola in her shoulders and hips.

It is nothing short of the ravings of a mad man if the questioner has been to the Cirque Medrano, and looked upon the clowns.   People have wondered how the actors of the Grosses Schauspielhaus could play to three audiences at once, the one in front, the one at the right, and the one at the left; here are the clowns playing to four.   It is not all slapstick either. There is almost no whacking in the clowns' own turns.   In these scenes they work out broad little comedy skits such as Ray and Johnny Dooley, Leon Errol and Walter Catlett, Eddie Cantor and George Le Maire, Willie and Eugene Howard, or Weber & Fields might offer in our revues.   The difference at the Medrano is that the actors seem to have consciously developed their gestures and their poses as supplementary expression to their faces.   Also they warily work round during their scenes, and give each part of the audience the benefit of both back and face.   The comedy of the Medrano is far funnier than the comedy of *The Follies* or the comedy of the Redoutensaal in Vienna; and not because the turns are broader.   It is

funnier because it is so intimately alive, because it is made with
all the actor's body, and because it is always directed at an audience.   Four audiences at once!   It is a priceless advantage.
The actor has always some one to press his art upon.   In our
theater half an actor's body is dead, or else vainly talking to the
scenery.   That is an understatement, if anything.   The only
way the actor can get directly at our audience, register upon it
the impact of his art, his personality, his emotion, is to turn
away from the scene and make his speech into a monologue.
That is the chief difficulty which stands in way of the sort of
acting which deals directly and frankly with the audience,
which admits that it is art and not reality, which says that the
actor is an actor and the audience is an actor, too; the kind of
acting, in short, which is called presentational in contrast to the
realistic method of representation which rules our theater.
On any stage that is surrounded by its audience, the player can
speak to his fellow-actor and to his audience at the same time.
In the Medrano it is no question of backs or faces.   The whole
man plays, and every inch of him has an audience.

There remains, however, the question of setting.   Clowns
need no atmosphere, but Hamlet must speak to a ghost.   An
acrobat is his own scenery, but Juliet needs a balcony.   Can the
Medrano manage such things?   Can this open ring do what
the stage of the Redoutensaal balks at?

The Medrano can do almost anything that our theater can do

—and a great many things more—because it can use the three essentials of setting and atmosphere: light, human bodies, and indications of place.

Light. . . . It is the fifth turn in the Cirque Medrano. Lydia *et* Henry, "Babies Dancers," two pitiable little children, who have been taught to do very bad imitations of their elders in the banal dances of the revues. After they have hopped and shaken their way uncertainly through two or three fox trots and shimmies, the great lights in the roof go out. Blackness, then a stain of amber in the center of the ring. The light brightens and the stain lengthens. It might fall upon the stone of an old cistern, if some one had thought to put it there. Then, when the figure of Salome crawls out along the stain, it would be many moments before we could see that it was the body of a four-year-old, whom some one had togged out with breast-plates. Or again darkness, and slowly a blue-green light from on high, and in the midst of it an Apache and a girl. It needs no curb, no lamp-post, no brick corner, to make the ring a moonlit street.

After light, there comes the human body. The Medrano as a circus does nothing to show how the actors themselves can make a setting. Why should it? But I remember the project of an American artist, in 1914, to put *The Cenci* upon the stage of a prize ring, and I remember how the sketches showed a chorus of human figures in costumes and with staves, circling

An impression of the Cirque Medrano in Paris.

about the people of Shelley's play and forming a dozen frames to the drama within.

After light and a setting of bodies comes just as much of the ordinary plastic scenery of the stage as you need, and just as little as you can get along with. If you care to dig a bit under the ring, and install machinery that will lower the floor in sections, pile up hills in concentric circles or even lift a throne or a well or an altar into the middle of the circus while the lights are out—well, there is nothing to prevent you. Juliet's balcony may hang above one of the entrances; or in the center of the stage throughout the whole action of *Les Fourberies de Scapin* may stand the *tréteau* or block, which Copeau makes the center of the action at the Vieux-Colombier. Scenically the problem of the Medrano is the most fascinating problem of the stage artist, the creation of a single permanent structure, large or small, which can stand throughout a play and give significant aid to the various scenes.

It is no such difficult task to imagine productions in the Medrano as it is to find plays for the Redoutensaal. The accompanying sketch shows an arrangement for *The Merchant of Venice*. Glowing Venetian lanterns are hung in the spaces between the arches at the top of the theater. The four entrances for the public are made entrances for the players as well. Below each gate is a double stair, railed at the top with Venetian iron. Between the stairs are benches, again in the shape of the period. The railings become the copings of the Rialto. The casket scenes are played in the center of the arena, while Portia and Nerissa watch the proceedings from a bench at one side; another bench seats the judges in the courtroom. Jessica leans out from an entrance to flirt with her lover, and the carnival mob chases old Shylock up and down the little stairs, over the benches, round about and out one of the two lower gates to the ring.

The ghost scene in *Hamlet?* Imagine the sentinel's companions moonlit in the center. Imagine a gallery behind the arches lighted with a dim and ghostly radiance. And imagine Marcellus suddenly and fearfully pointing to the figure of the dead man where it moves above the last row of spectators. No mixing of actors and audience, but what a thrill to see the ghost across a gulf of turned and straining faces, what a horror to see him over your own shoulder! Later Hamlet climbs stone by stone to meet and speak with the ghost from a platform above one of the great entrances.

The Jest—its prison scene? A block in the middle of the ring, a single glaring light from straight above, and the figure of Neri chained to the block.

Masse-Mensch? But a mob-play is too easy. The scene of the defeat, for instance; light upon the steps in the middle of the ring, workers piled up on it, messengers and refugees running in from gate after gate, from all four entrances, flinging

208

The Merchant of Venice as it might be given in the Cirque Medrano.

themselves back on the crowd in the center as the news of fresh disaster comes. The rattle of firearms; lights against the back of the high gallery, and the silhouettes of a score of machine guns trained on the actors and the audience.

It would be foolish to deny that the Medrano is not a theater for every play. It could not hold some that the artificiality of the Redoutensaal would make welcome—Oscar Wilde's, for instance—along with most of the conversational Realism of the past thirty years. But it could house all that the Grosses Schauspielhaus is fitted for—Greek tragedy and comedy, Shakespeare's greatest plays, dramas like *Florian Geyer*, *The Weavers*, and *Danton*. Some of the scenes of such pieces, the intimate episodes which Reinhardt's circus balks at, could be done excellently in the Medrano. It has all the intimacy of Copeau's theater, and it could bring into its ring many dramas of to-day,—*The Emperor Jones, Strife,*—which are impossible in the Vieux-Colombier. The Medrano has its limitations, of course, but they are not the limitations of size, emotion, or period. The plays that it could not do would be the plays least worth doing, at their best the plays which give to a reader almost all that they have to give.

If you should try to make a comparison of method, rather than of limitations, between the three active presentational theaters of Europe, and the fourth that might be, it would run, I think something like this: The Grosses Schauspielhaus tries to

209

deceive you in curious ways,—with dome and scenery and cloud machine. The Vieux-Colombier carefully explains to you that this is a theater, and that this is also life. The Redoutensaal asks you to dress up and see something artistic. The Medrano unites you and overwhelms you.

The thing that impresses any one who studies the Medrano from the point of view of play production—it may even impress the reader who tries to understand and sympathize with these attempts to suggest how plays might be produced there—is the great variety which such a theater offers and always the sense of unity which it creates. From every angle relationships center upon the actor, or cut across one another as he moves about, makes entrances or exits, or appears in the back of the audience. All these relationships work to a fine, natural unity. There is the actor in the center with the audience about him; there is the actor on the rim drawing the audience out and across to him. There are three circles of action within one another in a single unity. And there is the sense of all this which the audience has as it looks down, Olympian, from its banks of seats.

Something of the vision of the aeroplane invades the Medrano. We see life anew. We see it cut across on a fresh plane. Patterns appear of which we had no knowledge. Relationships become clear that were once confusion. We catch a sense of the roundness and rightness of life. And in the Medrano, while we win this vision in a new dimension, we do not lose the feel of the old. Such a theater establishes both for us. It gives us the three unities of space in all their fulness. They cut across one another like the planes of a hypercube. And the deeper they cut, the deeper grows the unity.

The Medrano seems to solve two problems of the modern theater. These arise from two desires in the leading directors and artists. One is to throw out the actor into sharp relief, stripped of everything but the essential in setting. This motivates a production like *Masse-Mensch*, with black curtains blotting out all but the center of the stage, and a theater like the Redoutensaal, with the actor placed amidst a background of formal and permanent beauty. The Medrano supplies a living background, the background of the audience itself. It is the background of life instead of death, a fulness of living things instead of the morbid emptiness of black curtains. It is a background more enveloping and animating than the ballroom of Maria Theresa. It is a background that accords with every mood, and is itself a unity.

The other problem is a psychological and a physical problem, the problem of life-principles in art. In the beginning the theater was masculine. Its essence was a thrust. The phallus was borne in the processional ritual at the opening of the Theater of Dionysus each spring; and its presence was significant. The greatest and the healthiest of the theaters have always plunged their actors into the midst of the audience. It is

211

only decadence, whether Roman or Victorian, that has withdrawn the actor into a sheath, a cave, a mouth, and has tried to drag the spirit of the spectator in with him. The peep show is essentially evil. I will not say it is feminine, but I will say that the art of the theater is a masculine art, that it is assertive and not receptive. Its business is to imbue the audience. It is not too difficult to see in the proscenium arch the reason for the barrenness of the realistic theater. Directors and artists who have felt this have tried to find a playhouse that lies nearer to the masculine vigor of Æschylus and Shakespeare. I think they can find it in the Cirque Medrano.

CHAPTER XVII

THE OLD SPIRIT—THE NEW THEATER

IT is hard to escape the belief that this ferment in the theater means something. Something for life and from life; something for art and from art. Something immensely important to the sense of godhead in man which is life and art together, life and art fecundating one another.

It seems peculiarly clear that the new forces in the theater have been working towards a spiritual change far more novel, far more interesting, and naturally far more important than any of the technical changes which they have brought about.

The technical changes have been confusing. First this business of scenic designers and revolving stages and all manner of show and mechanism; and now the "naked stage," abdication of the artist, scrapping of the machines, the actor alone, on a podium or in a circus ring. All in the name of drama.

There is only one explanation. These changes have come as part of an attempt to restore the theater to its old functions. They are two very extraordinary functions. One may be debauched into titillation, or may rise to that fulness of vitality, that excitation, upon which the second function of the theater is based, the function of exaltation.

Between the older theater, in which these functions worked as potently as they worked seldom, and the theater in which they may work again, lay the theater of Realism. It was a product of a tremendous force, a force for evil as well as good —the force of nineteenth century science. Science made the theater realistic and Realism made the drama scientific. It ceased to be a show. It became a photograph. The drama was made "truer," but only in the sense that a photograph may be truer to fact than a drawing by Picasso. It achieved resemblance to life. And then it ceased to have excitement or exaltation, because excitement, in the vivid sense in which I use it here, is most uncommon in modern life, and because exaltation is a rare and hidden thing showing seldom in outward relations. Both are too exceptional for Realism.

The restoration of excitement to the theater may appear to degrade it from the exact and austere report of life which Realism demands. But the thrill of movement and event is the element in the theater which lifts our spirits to the point where exaltation is possible. The power of the theater lies in just this ability to raise us to ecstasy through the love of vitality which is the commonest sign of divinity in life. And when the theater gives us ecstasy, what becomes of science? And who cares?

214

The new forces in the theater have struggled more or less blindly toward this end. They have tried beauty, richness, novelty, to win back excitement. They have only just begun to see that the liveliest excitation in the playhouse may come from the art of the actor and the art of the *régisseur* when they are stripped to the task of providing exaltation. Present the actor as an actor, and the background as an honest, material background, and you are ready for what glories the playwright and the peculiar genius of the theater can provide. The drama is free again for its eternal task—the showing of the soul of life.

Just how much this may mean is perhaps the test of your belief in the theater. It is the conviction of some of us that there has resided in the theater—and our hope that there may reside once more—something akin to the religious spirit. A definition of this spirit is difficult. It is certainly not religion. It goes behind religion. It is the exaltation of which formal creeds are a product. It is the vitality which informs life, and begets art. Out of the intensity of spiritual feeling which rises from the eternal processes of the universe and in turn becomes conscious of them, the thing is born which made Greek tragedy noble and which called drama back to life in the Middle Ages. Then it was the spirit of religion. To-day we might call it the spirit of life.

Both consciously and unconsciously men of the theater have sought to win back this exaltation. The latest attempt is in some ways the most daring and the most interesting. Max Reinhardt, leaving the playhouse, has tried to find it in a wedding of the drama and the church. Before this book is published, Reinhardt will have produced Calderon's mystic drama, *The Theater of the World*, under the high altar of the Collegienkirche in Salzburg. It is impossible now to speak of how far he has been able to effect an esthetic union between the handsome rococo edifice and the platform for his players; it is only possible to speculate on the spiritual feeling which spectators may gain through looking up at the actors from a flat floor, instead of looking down upon them. I cannot speak of the actual presence of exaltation in the audience, but we can speculate together on the possibilities of winning back spiritual vitality for the drama by union with the church.

First of all, there comes the disquieting thought that the theater presents the spectacle these days of a bird that lays eggs in another bird's nest. It isn't content with the one it has used for some centuries. It must go snooping about looking for a new haven for the drama. It tries the circus. It tries the ballroom. It shows us the Grosses Schauspielhaus and the Redoutensaal. It even seems to have got a notion of laying its eggs on the fourth wall. As this was the only thing that wasn't thoroughly real in the realistic theater, the result—the motion picture—is a bit of a scramble. And now the cuckoo theater has its eye on the church.

A truer charge might be that the human animal has a perverse liking for novelty; but even that could be countered with
the assertion that out of the stimulation of novelty, as out of
almost any stimulation, man can make art—if he has it in him.
As to that strange bird, the theater, it has never had good home-
keeping habits. It laid its eggs on Greek altars, and in the
mangers of Christian chapels. It nested in the inn yard in
England, and the tennis court in France. The fact that the
theater has a habit of roaming is worth about as much in this
discussion of its chance in the modern church as the fact that it
once found ecstasy by the Greek altar and produced little approaching dramatic literature while it was in the Christian
church.

Jacques Copeau complains that the drama has no home to-
day, and asserts that between the only choices open to it—the
church and the street—he much prefers the street. The
church doesn't want the drama; its creed doesn't want the
drama; its spirit repels the drama. In this relation of the
church and the theater there seems to be a problem for Europe
and a problem for America. The possibility of the two uniting
appears much greater in Europe. Europe—particularly
central and southern Europe, where Catholicism flourishes—
holds far more of genuine religious spirit than does America.
Moreover, the church there has the strength of tradition and of
art behind it. The esthetic-emotional grip of the churches

217

themselves, their architecture, their atmosphere, the sense of continuity that lives in them, holds men and women whose minds have rejected or ignored the authority of dogma. Even an American cut off from the traditional side of this life would feel a thrill in a drama in the Collegienkirche in Salzburg or in the Cathedral of Chartres that no performance in a theater could give him. The beauty of the ages would bless the drama in almost any European building except a theater. But come to America, and try to imagine *Everyman* in Trinity Church at the head of Wall street, or *The Theater of the World* in the Cathedral of St. John the Divine, not to bring it down to the level of a Methodist meeting house. The theater can always make religion more dramatic; witness the experiments of the Reverend William Norman Guthrie and Claude Bragdon with lighting and dance in St. Mark's-in-the-Bouwerie. But I do not think that any American church short of some Spanish-Indian mission in the Southwest can make the drama more religious.

For America—and, I suspect, for Europe, too—the problem is to find a way to the religious spirit independent of the church. It is not a question of producing plays in cathedrals, but of producing the spirit of life in plays. It is not: Can religion make itself theatrical? But: Can the theater make itself—in a new sense—religious?

If modern life, particularly the life of America, were spirit-

ual in any degree, all this would be simple.   Church and theater would both minister—as neither of them does now—to the
life of the spirit.   America has no art and no religion which
can make drama religious.   America does not believe, in any
deep sense.   Science has shattered dogma, and formal religion
has not been able to absorb an artistic or a philosophic spirit
great enough to recreate the religious spirit in men.

The thing is still more difficult because there is nowhere in
this country—unless, again, it is in the Southwest—a sense
of the age-long processes of life, which are part of the soil and
which leave their mark on men and women through the physical things that have always cradled them.   In Europe even the
cities hold this ancient and natural aspect; they are shaped by
man and time, even as the fields and the hills are shaped by
time and man.   These cities bask, and lie easy.   There is a
sense of long, slow growth in the very stones.   In America, it
is not only that our cities are new and brash.   Our countryside
is the same.   Even our farmhouses stick out of the land like
square boxes.   As simple a house in Europe has a breadth that
reconciles it with the sweep of the fields.   The American farm-
house is symbol of our separation from the soil.   We are out of
touch with the earthy vitality of life which might bring us at
least a little sense of the eternal.

If the man of the theater gives up the American church as a
path to the spirit of life, and if he finds no religion in modernity

219

from which to bring religion to the stage, what can he do? Is it possible that he can create the spiritual in the people by creating it in the theater? Can he see the vision himself; and, if he sees it and embodies it, can it make over the people?

Clive Bell, writing in *Art*, has described how such artists as William Blake and a very few others have reached the spiritual reality of existence—the thing we should call religion—directly, by pure intuition: "Some artists seem to have come at it by sheer force of imagination, unaided by anything without them; they have needed no material ladder to help them out of matter. They have spoken with reality as mind to mind."

Vision of this sort is so inordinately rare, that it seems as though some other way must be found to open spiritual truth to the artist of the theater. The only other way is through the deepest understanding of life itself. What can the artist find in American life to bring the vision? Nothing, surely, on the surface. Our architects have reached a more noteworthy expression than perhaps any of our painters, because they have somehow managed to identify themselves with a spirit of affirmation behind those industrial forms that our commercial imperialism presents to view in our men of position like Morgan and Ford, our periodicals like *The American Magazine* and *The Saturday Evening Post*, our subways and our cigarette ads, our patent medicines and our Kuppenheimer clothes.

The artist of the theater who is to create ecstasy by finding it, must see deeper than the architects behind the shams of American life. He must grasp the Spirit of America in a sense so extraordinary that the use we ordinarily make of that phrase will seem impossibly and blasphemously cheap. We have hints of what the artist must see and understand in Sandburg's sense of Chicago, in Vachel Lindsay's sense of the Middle West, in Waldo Frank's sense of New Mexico.

When theatrical genius has grasped the truth of America, it must be his business to make of himself and his theater a magnifying glass for the rest of his fellows. What he has been able to seize by sheer intuition, he must put in such form that it can seize all America. It is the hope of the theater that it can make the vision of one man become the vision of many.

There is no reason why a man of the theater should not have the vision; it has come to other artists. They have been able to transfer some share of it to the sensitive, the developed, the intellectual. The artist of the theater can perhaps transfer it to millions, to the uneducated and the dull, as well as to the receptive. In the theater he has a very extraordinary instrument. It is the art nearest to life; its material is almost life itself. This physical identity which it has with our very existence is the thing that can enable the artist to visualize with amazing intensity a religious spirit of which he has sensed only the faintest indications in life. He can create a world which shines with exaltation and which seems—as it indeed is—a

221

world of reality. He can give the spirit a pervading presence in the theater which it once had in the life of the Greeks and of the people of the Middle Ages. And when men and women see eternal spirit in such a form, who can say that they will not take it to them?

THE END

INDEX

INDEX

In the case of a number of plays listed in this index, the names of the director and the artist responsible for the particular production in question are coupled in a parenthesis preceding the numbers of the pages on which the production is mentioned; a semi-colon separates references to such special productions from references to the play alone. In the case of theaters listed, the name of the city in which each is located appears in parenthesis.

225

INDEX

INDEX

INDEX

Grieg, Edward, 54.
Grosses Schauspielhaus (Berlin), vii, 53, 55, 109, 110, 111, 115, 116, 164-170, opp. 164, opp. 168, 176, 177, 182, 189, 200, 204, 209-210, 216.
Grossi and Coquette, 203.
Grumpy, 83.
Grünewald, Isaac, 121-123, opp. 120, 122.
Guthrie, Rev. Wm. N., 218.

Hairy Ape, The, 5, 21, 29, 38.
Hamlet, 24; (Reinhardt-Stern) 110, 111, 168; 192, 208.
Hartau, Ludwig, 89.
Hasait, Max, 60, 61, 65, 72, 74, 116.
Hasenclever, Walter, 32, 33, 63.
Hauptmann, Gerhart, 5, 86, 162.
He Who Gets Slapped, (Pitoëff) opp. 24, 25; 98; (Simonson) 133.
Hebbel, 168.
Heims, Elsa, 82.
Heinrich, Sebastien, 186, 187.
Heinz, Wolfgang, 89.
Herford, Beatrice, 102.
Herterich, 84.
Hettner, Otto, 65.
Hilar, K. H., 34.
Hindemith, Paul, 32.
Hofmannsthal, Hugo von, 116, 121.
Hoftheater (Munich), see Munich National Theater.
Hopkins, Arthur, 14, 44, 129.
Howard, Eugene, 204.
Howard, Willie, 204.
Hume, Sam, 194.

Ibsen, Henrik, 6, 27, 29, 41.
Idle Inn, The, 94.
Ingalls, H. C., 46.

Inner proscenium, 64, 73.
Insect Comedy, The, (Hilar-Capek) 34-36.
International Theater Exhibition (Amsterdam and London), ix, x.
Irving, Sir Henry, 121.

Jannings, Emil, 82.
Jansson, Thoroff, 121.
Jaques-Dalcroze, see Dalcroze.
Jenseits, (Linnebach) 33, 63, 73.
Jessner, Leopold, vii, 78, 80, 88, 89, 119, opp. 126, opp. 128, opp. 130, opp. 132, opp. 134, 130-143, opp. 136, opp. 138, opp. 140, opp. 142, opp. 144, opp. 146, 147, 154-155, 175, 196.
Jest, The, 208.
Jolson, Al, 101.
Jones, Inigo, 120.
Josephine, 192.
Jouvet, Louis, 103, 104, 174, opp. 174, 176, 177, 180, opp. 180, 181, 182, 204.
Joyce, James, 66.
Judith, 168-169, opp. 168.
Julius Cæsar, (Reinhardt-Stern) 168; 193.

Kain, (Roller) 56.
Kaiser, Georg, 7, 32, 78.
Kaiser Heinrich VI, (Linnebach) 73.
Kamerny Theater (Moscow), 104.
Kammerspielhaus (Berlin), 46.
Katchaloff, V. I., 11.
Kaufman, Oskar, 45, 46, 146.
Kellerhals, Richard, 86, 87, 102.
Kemble, Chas., 23.
Klein, Cesar, opp. 126.
Knipper, Mme. O. L., 11, 12-13.
Kokoschka, Oskar, 32-33.

228

INDEX

229

INDEX

INDEX

231

INDEX

INDEX